A Church Beyond Belief

The Search for Belonging and the Religious Future

WILLIAM L. SACHS *and* MICHAEL S. BOS

Morehouse Publishing
NEW YORK

Morehouse Publishing, 4785 Linglestown Road, Suite 101, Harrisburg, PA 17112
Morehouse Publishing, 19 East 34th Street, New York, NY 10016
Morehouse Publishing is an imprint of Church Publishing Incorporated.

www.churchpublishing.org

Cover design by Laurie Klein Westhafer
Typeset by Denise Hoff

Library of Congress Cataloging-in-Publication Data

Sachs, William L., 1947–
    A church beyond belief : the search for belonging and the religious future / William L. Sachs and Michael S. Bos.
        pages cm
    ISBN 978-0-8192-2899-4 (pbk.)—ISBN 978-0-8192-2900-7 (ebook)
1. Church work with young adults.   2. Non-church-affiliated people.
3. Identification (Religion) 4. Psychology, Religious.   I. Title.
    BV4447.S225 2014
    253—dc23

                                                                2014004900

Printed in the United States of America

Contents

Acknowledgments

The creation of a book brings a special opportunity for gratitude. Ideas and information that reflect people's lives merit trust and careful presentation. We are grateful for the candor of various people who have described turning points in their lives. Their honest searches bring needed encouragement to us all.

More readily identified, key people have helped to bring the idea of this book to its fruition in print: Our publisher, Davis Perkins, for his encouragement in developing the theme of this book. He provided support in pressing boundaries of traditional thinking, and his interest and insight help give shape to our thoughts.

Our spouses, Austin Tucker and Tena Bos, whose support and partnership helped us hone the topic by graciously listening to us process ideas well beyond the boundaries of natural interest.

Our congregations, St. Stephens Church, Richmond, Virginia, and West End Collegiate Church, New York, New York, for being churches beyond belief. They are communities in which we have experienced the beauty of belonging, inspiring us to write this book.

We are thankful for them and the many others who supported us along the way.

William L. Sachs and Michael S. Bos

Ashley Visits Congregations

I

One Sunday morning it occurred to Ashley that she might visit a church. As she awakened, the thought lingered—it amused her. She smiled as coffee finished brewing and she poured a cup. Once visiting a church had been the farthest thing from her mind. Faith seemed like a crutch for the old and weak. Churches seemed irrelevant. Now she was exploring them.

As a student Ashley was confident of her abilities and certain of her future. She moved smoothly through high school and entered a good college. There she began to envision a career and her personal life. Graduation was followed by a job where she began to advance. The young man she had dated became her husband. The world was set, just as Ashley intended.

But Ashley's world did not become what she had expected. The happiness she anticipated never materialized. For reasons she was still sorting out, both she and her husband had affairs. Counseling did not help, they divorced, and disappeared quickly from each other's lives. "It's the only thing we did well," she mused. "We had nothing spiritual in common," she thought often.

Ashley paused again at the word "spiritual." As she sipped coffee, she tried to remember when "spiritual" matters gained priority and even what the word meant to her. Was it when she lost her job, or when she joined a women's book group? Did "spirituality" awaken when a new job took her across the country? She handled the job fine, but her personal life almost came unglued. Involvement with a married man and evenings with scotch became a downward spiral. Comments at work about sloppy performance struck home. She ended both destructive ties.

Along the way "spirituality" became a key reference point. But more questions than answers surfaced: What did she believe and where did she belong? As these questions bore in on her, Ashley knew she needed to search, and as she searched the questions intensified. Was she alone or were there other people facing similar challenges? Was there something she could believe in that could give her deep roots in life? Was there something beyond her vague, agnostic existence? Was there a group of people with whom she might seek answers together? As these questions came into focus, the thought of attending a church first crossed Ashley's mind.

Initially the thought surprised her. It was uncomfortable and odd. A church? At first Ashley doubted there could be a congregation for her. Laughing at this bizarre idea, several friends discouraged her. The images of churches were not appealing. Ashley imagined stern morality and threats of eternal judgment. She imagined being coerced to believe ideas that were absurd or to take sides in disputes that seemed pointless. Ashley wanted belief and belonging churches did not seem likely to offer. But she resolved to explore a few congregations. Telling no one, and hoping not to be recognized, she set off one cold Sunday morning.

She arrived at a modern building more like a theatre than a church. People seemed friendly; she was greeted several times while making her way to the sanctuary, and relaxed as she saw people of all ages. As the service began, a band played contemporary music. "Is this really a church?" she asked herself. When the pastor took the stage in a polo shirt, her interest piqued. Then he began his sermon on finding direction in life. This didn't seem like sermons she remembered. It was about real life, filled with humor, and had a practical, encouraging message. As Ashley listened to the sermon, hope surfaced. This could be exactly what she needed.

Ashley continued attending, even joining a small group in her neighborhood. However, things became uncomfortable for her. What felt like an open and friendly environment started to feel restrictive. The problem crystalized for her during a meeting with her small group. When she mentioned she was dating a man from another faith, disapproval was palpable. Questions soon emerged: Would he become a Christian? Was there any chance he would be saved?

Ashley wasn't sure how to answer. Frankly, she had never thought about "being saved" before. She realized there was a sense in this congregation that there were those who were true believers, and there were those who were not and would suffer eternally. Ashley soon stopped attending. At first this congregation offered a dynamic path to faith and life. But as she became involved, Ashley realized these were rigid, conservative beliefs repackaged for greater appeal.

Several weeks of quiet Sundays went by and Ashley took solace in her book group and in private time. But the nagging feeling would not go away. She could respect the conservative approach: there was something clear and confident about it. But she could not accept the ideas that were pressed upon her, and the readiness to exclude people who were different dismayed her. She also feared the need for wholesale adoption of their beliefs if she wanted to belong. Clearly this sort of congregation was not for her. But she needed to belong.

Quiet inquiries among friends brought up the name of another congregation, not far away physically, but apparently quite different otherwise. She resolved to visit there, intent on finding the place where she could belong. A bright Sunday morning seemed ideal and off she went.

The Gothic structure communicated sound, spiritual roots. Ashley had become intrigued by the word "tradition," and this structure resonated with her image of it. Ashley wanted to feel a part of something larger, older, truer than what she had ever known. She wanted something that had been tested by time and survived. Gothic architecture seemed laden with experience and truth. Perhaps she would find them for herself in this congregation, starting this Sunday morning.

Arriving before the worship service began, she encountered a greeter, a friendly woman who handed her a leaflet and gestured toward a pew. Taking a seat Ashley liked the atmosphere she discovered. A soft organ prelude created an air of reverence that she found appealing. She liked the note of formality that accompanied the worship. The choir and ministers wore robes and entered in a procession up the long aisle. The service was not easy to follow, though Ashley liked the lessons read and prayers offered. There was a deeply spiritual sense that Ashley liked.

She also liked the fact that women and men shared in leading worship. She was pleased when a woman climbed into the pulpit to give the sermon. At first the message spoke deeply to her. There was a depth of personal conviction and a compassionate view of life that Ashley readily endorsed. The religious views were different from the previous congregation.

Now there was talk of justice and inclusion, and an insistence on taking practical steps to achieve them.

But there was also the impression that if you were on the wrong side of history, you would harm others and suffer yourself. This emphasis surprised Ashley and she wondered how the minister's faith could justify such rigidity in the name of inclusion. Doubt was honored and spiritual searches were welcome, if they leaned in the desired theological direction.

Still, the minister's message was intriguing. Studying the service leaflet she decided to attend an adult class that would begin after the service ended. Another greeter showed her the way and in a large room she discovered that a reception preceded what would be the class. As she entered the room, people whizzed past her, a few smiling as they raced, most intent on their destinations. At a wide table Ashley took a cup of coffee and turned to view the room.

Perhaps one hundred people were there, gathered in small clusters, smiling and animated. Ashley edged toward one cluster. Maybe she could introduce herself and join the conversation. But there seemed to be no entry point. She overheard references to family events and children's achievements to which she could not relate. Feeling awkward, she eased toward another cluster of people. But there she overheard what seemed like a foreign language. She realized this must be a discussion of church meetings and programs. It washed completely over her. There were references to programs and resolutions at church conferences that meant nothing to her.

Again people smiled at one another and seemed deeply engaged. But they failed to notice her. She felt a slight desperation building within; she thought she could be a part of things there, for many of the external features touched her. But how could she get into the circle and make sense of this institutional religious talk?

The educational program that morning did not relieve her desperation. It began well and briefly revived her interest. A panel discussed healthcare needs of poor people in the city and suggested what this meant in religious terms. "That makes sense," Ashley thought. One panelist referred to the spiritual needs of the poor and of those who work with them. This emphasis on practical help grounded in personal spirituality touched her deeply. Although no one had spoken to her, there was something here to guide her. Here she might learn to help people in need.

Then the open door that had beckoned to her closed. Panel members detailed the congregation's support for programs of their denomination. Much emphasis was placed on the generosity of the budget; but how it benefitted people in need seemed lost in references to institutional structures. The spiritual dimension succumbed to a programmatic outlook Ashley could not understand.

> We are psychologically, emotionally, cognitively, and spiritually hardwired for connection, love, and belonging. Connection, along with love and belonging (two expressions of connection), is why we are here, and it is what gives purpose and meaning to our lives.
>
> **Brené Brown**
>
> *Daring Greatly: How the Courage to Be Vulnerable Transforms the Way We Live, Love, Parent, and Lead*

When a panelist dwelt on a position paper and a resolution at denomination headquarters, Ashley was ready to leave. Again she had made a wrong turn. Much of what she found there was appealing. But she felt like an interloper at events meant for others. No one spoke to her, much less offered to explain what they were discussing. The people seemed interested in much that she was interested in, but they were not interested in her.

There is more at stake than whether or not the Ashleys of our world find a church home. What about the state in which people are left after their experience in a church? Brené Brown has helped shape our understanding of this problem by differentiating between "belonging" and "fitting in." She defines it this way: "Fitting in is about assessing a situation and becoming who you need to be in order to be accepted. Belonging, on the other hand, doesn't require us to change who we are; it requires us to be who we are."[1] When we don't fit in, we believe there must be something wrong with us. We are left feeling shame and unworthy of love and belonging.

Unfortunately, too many churches are better at creating experiences of shame and disconnection rather than connection and belonging. Today the sacred space people seek is a place where they can be vulnerable about who they are and where they are in life. But what they often find is pressure to change or hide who they are so that they can fit in.

We felt compelled to write this book because too many people have been wounded in the wake of seeking to fit in. This book is for those who yearn to move beyond fitting in and create a community where true belonging can be experienced. It is for clergy and lay leaders, Sunday school teachers and denominational staff. It is for all who struggle with what it means to make the church a place where people can be seen for who they are and where they are in life, and know there is a place for them.

II

In this book we describe the new pattern of belonging that is demanded of America's congregations, and we offer discouraging commentary on their ability to offer it. For a number of people old assumptions of membership are being replaced by spiritual criteria of participation. People now are seeking community and companionship. Many are young adults whose life situations reflect upheaval and mobility. But persons of all ages see themselves on spiritual journeys fueled by insistent new questions. They seek fresh, practical perspective on belief and faith tradition. They are bringing new criteria of faith community.

While having high expectations of congregations, they have little interest in habitual religious approaches. They will not accept being an institutional program or category. They will not follow a prescribed path toward being an authentic believer. They do not automatically respond to leaders because of the office they hold or the institution they serve. Instead they look for personal guidance from those whose quality of life embodies the ideals of faith. They refuse to be caught up in partisan religious and "culture wars" disputes, instead looking to religious life as a way of transcending if not resolving conflicts.

Similarly, Ashley and her counterparts are inherently fascinated by religious pluralism and accepting of it. They do not see a contest between faiths; instead they seek ways to learn from various faiths and to affirm, rather than exclude or dismiss, followers of them. Ashley would say that people must embrace pluralism because of what they believe, not in spite of it.

As a result spiritually motivated people look to congregations for a novel alignment of faith and life, belief and belonging. To take such a step, congregations must pursue an adaptive strategy that will not ignore the priorities that absorb their energies but will meld spiritual criteria to them. We believe that an adaptive strategy of this sort is likely to fuel congregational growth.

Such a strategy hinges on a revised approach to participation and a readiness to embrace new people and priorities.

A fresh focus on incorporation, formation, and personal and shared vocation must be offered. The challenge for congregations is to approach their local contexts innovatively. Congregational leaders must live in two worlds, for they cannot simply cast aside old assumptions; many congregational members continue to be guided by older assumptions they will have difficulty modifying.

Yet congregations and their leaders must remember that an irreversible shift is underway in how people seek to belong. Increasingly people are no longer willing to adopt beliefs as a prerequisite to belong. Instead, they seek to belong well before they know what they believe—if they ever have definitive beliefs! Most congregations approach belief and belonging in ways that present barriers to a new generation.

As a result churches have lost the influence to insist that people follow old patterns of belonging. People are no longer motivated by cultural or kinship pressures to conform. They are experiencing the freedom to choose their own religious pathways—or none at all. And with this freedom comes new criteria. Their search is driven by a deep longing to unite separated aspects of life in community with others. It focuses on new alignments of personal search, faith tradition, and local community. There is a profound intention of creating new bonds, grounded in tradition, where faith helps people flourish, and their shared life is committed to serve others in ways that change lives. Past programs have sought to answer this challenge with "one size fits all," but a new generation embraces a pluralism of paths within Christianity and the local church—just as it does with people. Their impulse is to use these paths as sources for their own spiritual journeys.

This is not the first time people have embarked on such a search or congregations have faced such a challenge. From ancient times to the present there are continuing instances of people on spiritual journeys and religious institutions challenged to respond. Now there are new patterns to this search and congregations often overlook them in their focus on institutional demands. The current spiritual ferment forces congregations to ask uncomfortable questions: Where do they intend to take people? For what way of life are people being formed? And the most difficult question: What is distinctive about the mission of congregations today? One thing is certain for Ashley: if the overarching goal is simply a church's survival, she is not convinced the church is worth saving. Congregations must address these questions, but not in distracting, institutional ways. As congregations become internally absorbed, people like Ashley wonder if there is a place where they can make sense of spirituality and life. Where can they belong?

Ashley did not consider her role in a larger trend. All she knew was the urgency of her own search. After her disappointing visits, a few weeks passed with Ashley keeping quietly to herself. She focused on work, her discussion group, and quiet time. Congregations seemed far removed from her life and what she sought. Either they were strident, or they were obsessed with institutional approaches. Either a congregation wanted to coerce her into accepting narrow beliefs or it did little to welcome her, much less appreciate her faith journey.

Bits of her church exposure had resonated. The conservative congregation's clarity and forthrightness were striking, but the views appalled her. The progressive congregation conveyed openness to current issues that she welcomed. But liberals seemed enamored with questions while being short of answers, and conservatives focused on rigid answers that allowed little room for questions. There seemed no place for her in either congregation. There was too much in the way to give her the feeling of belonging.

Still her need to belong persisted. She had unanswered questions about faith, spirituality, and life itself. She thought of herself as a good person. But why had life taken the turns

she had experienced? She knew she was assertive and independent; yet she was realizing that she needed to be part of
a group grounded in tradition and belief where prayer and
meditation might make sense. Several friends thought she
was crazy, but others encouraged her search.

She needed a place where she could learn with others and
learn to help others. It would be a place where her experiences would make sense and where she could find hope in a
future she could share with valued friends. Perhaps the circle
of smiling people would include her. Perhaps the strange language of programs and committees might make sense, and
she might even care. Perhaps she would visit a church again.

III

There are many people of all ages like Ashley today and the
number is increasing. They are neither steeped in religious life
nor alienated from it. Some were raised in religious faiths and
drifted away. There are also those who have little religious background at all. In every case, they reached adulthood and found
their assumptions about life were inadequate. They prized
their independence and resisted the feeling of being told what
to believe and do. They thought of themselves as open to wider
frames of culture and belief. They could be critical of any religious or political system that seemed an affront to their independence. But independence and an open spirit alone could
not grasp the sorts of life issues they inevitably began to face.

Meanwhile congregations have relied upon people living
settled lives. Even those congregations that are open to single
people, and to gay and partnered people, have presumed a
settled life in the context where the congregation is located.
Congregations think of themselves as having ministries to
people who reflect a particular way of life. But they may be stuck
in outdated assumptions about their people and their setting.

For persons without roots in that location, and for persons living mobile lives as work may dictate, entry into a congregation becomes daunting. In many cases only lengthy residence in a community legitimates recognition by the congregation. For people who have moved, or whose lives have been disrupted emotionally and professionally, congregations may not extend themselves. Ministries to people in crisis flow more readily when the person and the family are already acknowledged by the congregation.

For people like Ashley, with little faith background and a series of personal jolts, there is little sense of where to turn. Core questions of identity and purpose press in on her. Who is she? What does she believe? How can she make sense of a life she never imagined, in a place she never envisioned, after losses she cannot explain, having found herself shaken thoroughly? As she explored further, Ashley was not at all certain what she believed or where she stood. For whom or what would she become an advocate? What would she do to make the world a better place? Where could she turn? Was there a place where she could address these questions in the company of people who grasped the depth of her search for answers? Where could she belong?

If these are the questions that Ashley and people like her are bringing to congregations, what questions are congregations asking? Is there any meeting ground, or could there be? When one surveys the issues in American religious life, there seems to be little basis for encouragement. From the news media one concludes that religion and conflict go together. There have been sexual and financial scandals that have gotten publicity out of proportion to their prevalence. Some people have been deeply hurt by such misconduct and trust in religious life has eroded.

America's religious institutions, especially its Christian majority, have also suffered a widespread, self-inflicted wound.

For a generation they have been locked in a "culture war." Conservatives, often referring to themselves as "orthodox" or "traditionalist," have mobilized to defend beliefs and moral values that, in their view, have been imperiled. A seemingly godless, secular culture has seized cultural control through domination of the media. Destructive images featuring casual sex, alcohol consumption, self-indulgence, acceptance of anomalous lifestyles, and drug usage have been displayed. Liberal Christianity, bent on cultural accommodation, has been complicit and so represents betrayal. While divided on theological issues and aspects of religious heritage, conservatives intend to save America from a moral and religious abyss.

Though liberals celebrate the larger culture's embrace of progressive ideals on justice and morality, they continue their struggle against religious, political, and social conservatism, which are seen as denying God's dream for the world. Any agenda that excludes or marginalizes persons or groups, whether LGBT persons or illegal immigrants, denies God's love of all people. But the result has been a tension that has polarized Christians, creating disdain for those who differ. The Ashleys of today sense that any group using disdain or demonization as a requisite for acceptance does not offer genuine belonging. It is a clue that the belonging she seeks is absent.

> Regular churchgoing, moreover, now correlates even more strongly with some types of political and social conservatism than it did several decades ago. . . . The most and least religiously active people are further apart attitudinally than they were several decades ago, but this trend does not warrant a declaration of culture war—yet.
>
> **Mark Chaves**
>
> *American Religion*

It is apparent that while culture wars and scandals have dominated coverage of religion, a deeper reality is definitive. In part this reflects strained economic realities. In part it reflects the withering of centralized religious authority and institutional life. Religious pluralism now blurs historic religious identities while mobility and shifting demographics challenge assumptions about religion's role in local contexts. Meanwhile fewer people adhere to the faith in which they were raised and increasing numbers are raised in no faith at all. Congregations are challenged to form believers who grow into leadership roles to guide their ministries. Aging populations of lay leaders and difficulties in finding younger adults to succeed them intensify the disruption.

The root of conflict is confusion over leadership and mission. Most of religious America resists the extremes of liberalism and conservatism and the conflicts they have engendered. But if Ashley's experience and that of people like her is assessed closely, it becomes plain that the churches' life is not focused properly. Most of America's Christian congregations perceive a crisis of faith and life, but their responses would fail to reach the Ashleys in their midst. It can be difficult to distinguish many congregations from a social club or service organization. Religious leaders, lay and clergy, tend to measure their state in institutional terms such as membership, attendance, and budget. But statistics gloss over the issue of what makes them religious. The failure of many congregations to address this question leaves them wanting in Ashley's eyes.

Specifically, we note these impulses of many congregations that tend to distance themselves from people they say they wish to reach:

1. **They make beliefs more pronounced rather than the spiritual quest more profound.** Many congregations assume

that the foremost approach to perceptions of crisis is to become more sharply defined in their beliefs and practices, and so to demarcate themselves from perceived threats and opponents. But the result is that they do not appeal to many like Ashley who value spiritual breadth and do not want to take sides to fight straw men. And despite sharp emphasis on particular ideals, such as "social justice" or biblical literalism, many congregations fail to explain themselves to Ashley and her peers in ways they can respect and absorb.

2. **They make faith a binary choice.** Many congregations and denominations with which they are affiliated affirm that faith has somehow gone awry. Conservatives see liberal betrayal, for example, and liberals see conservative distortions of genuine religious belief and life. Both sides presume the power of the other to harm the lives of vulnerable people. But people like Ashley are unformed religiously. They hope to learn from a variety of perspectives, not to reject one in favor of the other.

3. **They make faith political.** The presumption of politics mixing with religion, again in adversarial terms, dismays the Ashleys in our society. They are not apolitical, and can readily engage in discussion and campaigning around favorite issues. But they will not give automatic support to one view or party. They resist being viewed as an age-group bloc and if pressed will emphasize their independence.

4. **They ignore pluralism.** References to firmly held belief, and to "tradition," or "mission," or "inclusion" have great appeal to many like Ashley. Such terms bespeak clarity and practical intention. But when clarity and firmness edge into rigidity and uncritical rejection of diversity and disagreement, the Ashleys begin to back away. Part of the religious response to perceptions of crisis has been a hard-edged toughness in the name of being clear. But the Ashleys seek a theological and practical process shaped collectively in

ways that unite diverse spiritual journeys into a fresh experience of faith community. They seek spiritual guidance from diverse sources, beyond the tradition that may be their primary allegiance.

5. **They enfold people as part of an institutional crowd rather than part of a spiritual community.** As a result, congregations allow themselves an institutional narcissism that heightens their practical irrelevance, even when people like Ashley knock on the door. For many congregations who readily welcome people, they rapidly move to incorporate visitors into existing programs and activities that can bear little relation to what motivated the visit. But people like Ashley who enter congregational doors do not intend simply to be members of a religious institution. They need a place that helps them to live with purpose and focus. They shun older notions of personal and social success to which many congregations remain wed. They seek faith community that is open to diverse personal journeys and able to call forth authentic, shared, unfolding spiritual life. The institutional obsessions of many leaders and congregations can overlook their urgent pursuit.

> According to the research by Percept Group, people are not seeking institutional leaders who tell them what to do. They desire leaders who "work with them on deciding what to do and then help them do it."

Some congregations have taken one or another kind of initiative. Some have found paid or volunteer staff members who might appeal to the Ashleys in their midst, while others have entertained new forms of spiritual engagement that break the rules and patterns of the past. Many of the leaders of innovative congregations began as youth leaders, where the openness to risk and experimentation is much greater than normally tolerated by a congregation. Those congregations that have taken such steps inevitably have benefitted and created new means for welcoming diverse sectors of their local communities. These represent important signs that when congregations dare to take thoughtful initiative, good results usually follow.

A few churches have embraced spiritual priorities and made important advances in incorporating people like Ashley. But if the influence of one large church, Willow Creek, outside Chicago, is evidence, the jury is out on how effectively congregations can build lasting spiritual growth. The topic is increasingly broached, but the results are inconclusive at best.

Even in circumstances where there has been concerted attention to current spiritual life, basic questions surface. How can congregations not only welcome but incorporate diverse people, especially those who seek novel spiritual journeys in a community? What can be done to form the faith of the Ashleys, and what manner of pastoral care will sustain them, especially if they encounter personal crisis? Will they be treated as unusual or separate in the congregation, or become part of the congregation's core? How can they be welcomed as they are and not taken to a predetermined state of mind and life, but invited into a living community of faith? How can they also be shaped as leaders to revive a congregation as it faces an uncertain future?

The tendency in most congregations is to approach Ashley and her peers in all or nothing terms. Either they will accept the congregation as it is, or there is little room for them. Alternatively, either the congregation must be remade entirely, or it will dissolve in irrelevance. Instead, as we shall discuss, balance is a key word. On the one hand, congregations must balance management of their life with innovative leadership. They must see that management is not the same as leadership, but is just as necessary. The one must be tangible, the other visionary: one must be tested and steady; the other must be open to innovation.

The Ashleys seek a balance that has eluded them. They seek an alignment of faith and life they cannot find on their own. Belief for them is linked inherently to belonging. The objective forms of belief must be balanced by subjective dimensions. Well-managed programs focused on their questions, and effectively bringing them in and shaping them, are welcome. Above all, the Ashleys seek to join with others in an effort to adapt religious tradition and congregational life to the new circumstances they embody. They are looking to leave a distinctive mark. They are looking to be living examples of the best of religious faith and life.

IV

But can the balance congregations must find, and the balance Ashley and her peers seek, be aligned somehow? We are not optimistic. For all the justifiable logic of the outlook of most congregational leaders, their removal from the concerns of the Ashleys is striking. Feeling backed into one or another corner, many leaders of congregations are in avid pursuit of carefully managed survival strategies. Worse, they are prone to grasp at promises of quick fund-raising or programmatic responses which usually create brief bursts of energy at best. Responses to the Ashleys of our time cannot be quick fixes. Circumstances call for innovative leadership.

Congregations today are challenged to look beyond assumptions and existing categories. This challenge, however, does not mean that congregations should abandon programs, patterns, and people they have found reliable. No dilution of faith and practice is implied. Ashley's openness and receptivity can work to the advantage of congregations, if they grasp the depth of her journey toward belonging.

It is clear that there is still time. Although the challenges of the Ashleys represent a historic crossroads for congregations, the window of opportunity remains open. Ashley's search for a congregation goes on. She has neither rejected congregations altogether nor endorsed their habitual patterns wholeheartedly. Congregations might adapt creatively to welcome the vitality Ashley might bring. But the nature of her openness requires that congregational leaders invite and incorporate her in certain new ways.

1. **Faith is not static belief but a dynamic journey.** The churches must be flexible and discursive in presenting their beliefs. Ashley's generation insists on open discussion and fair consideration of options. Convictions cannot be presented and will not be accepted whole. The basis and development of key faith tenets must be opened up in ways that people on spiritual journeys find accessible. Faith must be seen in dynamic, unfolding ways, not in static terms and categories. Congregations can no longer carry a single strand of Christian tradition. They must create the spiritual space in which diverse people can belong together and shape shared faith commitment together.

2. **From preserving the institution to promoting a faith that flourishes.** The dire perceptions of many congregational leaders about the state of faith and moral life must be balanced by a fresh sense of opportunity. More energy must go into creative initiative than into complaining or passive inertia. The attitudes of many faith leaders and communities are clouded by fear and dismay about the economy and the culture. Even if circumstances are as dire as some announce, the issue of what faith communities can do is not sufficiently addressed. Decrying contemporary life or

pretending not to notice it at all appeals to few who seek a congregational home. The Ashleys bring honest, searching, open-ended questions that demand substantial answers.

3. **It's about my life, not my vote.** Few would argue that religion should be divorced from politics or could be. But the mixture of religious people and institutions with political causes and figures blurs religious intentions, which effectively alienates many like Ashley. Religion loses its integrity when it makes solely political cause, even with noble intentions. Worse, religion can justify political power for the sake of power alone, and justify excluding those who disagree. Nothing could be further from the spiritual priorities Ashley and her peers hold. They are focused on identifying what religion and spirituality mean for a better life, not for political gain.

4. **Faith that doesn't entertain questions doesn't have answers.** Similarly, theological and practical intransigence do little to appeal to today's spiritual journey. To be sure, congregational leaders can cite a bevy of reasons for not varying from their familiar path. But no reason can distract from what has become a general lack of flexibility in congregational life and in the denominations they represent. If the level of crisis is indeed so great, the necessity for innovative leadership seems self-evident. In some congregations such signs are evident, but more often intransigence and denial prevail.

5. **The church must lose control.** No personal spiritual search is fueled or guided by the institutional self-absorption of most congregations and their leaders. Even while speaking of "leadership," they think in terms of management. Congregations will not absorb new people and their spiritual energies and life searches by management alone. Yet many congregations cling to rigid, narrowly institutional ideas, and are unclear about the religious nature of

their identity. They may say that spirituality is welcome, but their actions belie their words. Many leaders of congregations will complain that spirituality is vague and that newcomers must learn to appreciate congregational ways and prove themselves as members. Then answers to their questions will be apparent.

The preoccupations of congregational leaders are understandable. But they deny the validity of Ashley's issues. Ironically at a time when some congregations face membership loss and erosion of their leadership base, they ignore what would be a major resource. The reason is that the perceived price is too high. Alterations of habitual institutional outlooks and priorities seem too precious a sacrifice, even if this resistance blocks possibility. Too many people in congregations are intent on preserving their sense of prerogative rather than forging creative solutions to their challenges. The thought of incorporating people like Ashley eludes them.

It may seem that in pointing to membership loss as emblematic of the problem, we are implying that numerical growth is the outcome all should seek. Therefore we need to say a word about the lens with which we view this.

In Charles Van Engen's work *God's Missionary People*, he proposes that yearning for growth is a mark of the true church.[2] We agree with this, but not in the sense that a church should be utilitarian in approaches to raising its membership numbers, which is not implied in Van Engen's work, nor that ministry is about counting heads that are deemed "saved." What we propose is that a mark of the church is to care about people and yearn to do something of spiritual substance that helps an increasing number of people. Put another way, we should have a holy discontent that God can use us to do more for more people. Without this impetus, our sense of mission withers.

By framing it in this way, it is not the number of people in the pews that determines our faithfulness to our mission in the world. It is the size of the impact we make. And most importantly, we recognize that a congregation's impact isn't always reflected in increased attendance. There are many small congregations whose impact outsizes their attendance. Our hope from this book is simply this: that a focus on belonging helps congregations make a greater impact on a greater number of people. This work can take shape in small congregations and large ones, and in any number of unconventional means to respond to peoples' needs.

Which raises the important question: if congregations were to adapt, how would they do so? If people like Ashley were to find a congregation where they could belong, what would it look like? What do congregations need to understand and how do they need to see differently? What would they need to do effectively to forge a genuine appeal to today's spiritual journey?

The answers are not apparent. Today the landscape of religious life and many of the stirrings among congregations overflow with references to the Ashleys of this moment. There has been extended discussion of "spirituality" and "spiritual journeys" and "spiritual seekers." There have also been discussions of belonging, with little widespread impact. There have been initiatives to build fresh approaches to congregational life based on spiritual categories. But the relation of spirituality to belonging remains unclear, as Ashley's confused search reveals.

In addition, discussions of leadership have not tapped the perspective Ashley and her peers bring. Above all, congregations cannot assume that being a seeker is a temporary phase awaiting a traditional lifestyle and acceptance of firm belief. Instead congregations can see themselves as places of ongoing spiritual exploration. But this possibility seems remote. There is much to be reconceived if congregations are to make sense to Ashley and she to them.

In these pages we describe the new meaning of belonging that must take hold if congregational life is to be revitalized by people like Ashley. The central feature is a deep exploration of what faith tradition can mean in building vital forms of community today. Given the extent of "religious illiteracy," as one author puts it, this exploration is both challenge and opportunity. Yet the promise that looms is a new synthesis of faith and life, and a new surge of people seeking not only a personal faith but a shared one in ways that guide them effectively and benefit others.

To make this case, we turn in chapter one to consider the nature of the spirituality that is taking hold. There has been much discussion of people who are "spiritual seekers" and of such movements as the "emerging church" and the "missional church." The limits of individualism and consumerism are becoming clear. Congregations cannot ignore this widespread spiritual quest. We will make sense of this variety of movements. We will also probe the nature of "spiritual growth" today, noting who is involved and why such a quest has gained momentum.

Chapter two describes the disconnections of American life. Spiritually motivated people are being estranged from religious institutions while religious institutions lack clarity about their ends and means. Essentially, congregations lack clarity on where to take people today and by what means. If there are references today to being on a journey, what sort of journey and toward what destination? We will explain why congregations are preoccupied, and how people like Ashley can enliven them. Such disconnection has happened before. We show that spiritual energies, and congregational preoccupations, have precedents that can instruct.

Chapter three describes how belonging happens. It arises out of the realization that you cannot face life and its challenges alone. Ashley and her peers seek a setting where lasting ties can bind them together. They pursue the dream of personal authenticity. Yet they have realized that only shared authenticity fulfills their inner quests. The task for congregations is to reshape their lives for people who seek a pathway to authenticity.

Chapter four addresses the foremost question for many persons today: What do I believe? The pursuit of belonging is unfinished without cultivation of belief. They seek a middle ground where they can be rooted in basic tenets of faith, yet appreciative of the variety of belief. They discover that belief encourages a particular form of belonging which, in turn, shapes shared faith experience. Belief is the cornerstone of belonging. We will show how this happens today.

Chapter five considers the magic of communities that move beyond acceptance to relationships that effect change. They become communities of belonging that encourage common purpose that is reflected in a vocation for one's daily life. And they grow outward in care for people in need in one's context and beyond. This growth helps form healthy communities that add a new dimension to the mission of the church. Mission becomes more than what we can do "to" and "for" others; it is what we can do and who we can be "with" one another.

Chapter six describes how new norms of spirituality and spiritual community can unite people of different faiths and different cultures. Some of these people are within one's own faith tradition. For a growing number of people, belonging must entail diversity within community. As religious pluralism has reached new heights, it is challenging congregations to cultivate both a particularity and a plurality of faith options. Although seemly contradictory, such a joint affirmation is demanded of those who would lead creatively today.

The book's conclusion suggests the adaptive tasks now required of religious leaders. As we suggest throughout the book, an adaptive stance can be devised in life-giving ways. This book does not offer a formula for how to make such adaptations. Rather by explaining a major trend, we chart a new course for congregational life.

Can you and your congregation incorporate people on novel spiritual searches? A new approach is needed, focusing on a spiritually motivated approach to belonging. To the extent that congregations embrace a new spiritual journey, and that the Ashleys recognize their need for grounding, there could be a creative convergence, or even a dramatic shift in patterns of congregational life and effectiveness. For this to happen, the Ashleys and the congregations must both admit that they are enmeshed in spiritual journeys.

William Sachs and Michael Bos

CHAPTER ONE

She's Not Alone

The Urge to Fit In

Until crises she could not have imagined began to reshape her life, Ashley would have laughed at the idea that she was simply trying to fit in. She thought of herself as assertive and independent. She could be the life of the party and did not mind being outrageous. Looking back on high school and college years, she wondered that she avoided lasting consequences. By some instinct she stopped short of risky behavior. She gave the impression of being more adventurous than she was. She could smile at her antics while wondering how she slid past serious trouble.

She had wanted to be a rebel, at least by night, and productive enough by day to get ahead in life. She succeeded and for a while could proclaim loudly that she was free to do as she pleased. She made this point to her parents and reinforced it by her behavior with friends. Later she marveled there was not more conflict at home. Now well into adulthood and beginning to imagine how it would feel to be thirty, she could still declare her independence, while admitting to herself that she was not certain what this meant. The aggressive edge had softened. Too much had occurred. Life was not so simple. Freedom had complexities and limits.

Now Ashley was looking for something she never dreamed would be missing: a place and a group of people where she felt she belonged. Growing up she could take it for granted even as she pushed back at her world. She was starting to grasp that as a child and even as a rebellious teenager, being accepted had been her intense hope. She barely knew how much this mattered at the time, and would have been enraged if anyone suggested it. But the therapy that followed divorce began to open her eyes. She finally admitted to herself, though as yet to no one else, that all she ever wanted was to belong. Growing up, this had meant desperately trying to fit in. Belonging in a significant way meant only that: fitting in.

She wanted to be liked, maybe even admired, when she was younger. She called attention to herself in the hope of being acceptable. Peer approval meant the world to Ashley. As college and work expanded her life, the urge to fit in—to be acceptable to others—intensified. Beneath her façade was a young woman who needed to know she had a place in the world and who was not sure she did. She longed to find the setting in which she felt understood and welcomed. That was her pursuit, above all others. And it still was, even though she had been chastened by life. "The scary thing is," she mused, "I want to be real and I'm not sure I know how."

Who was the authentic Ashley? She was still discovering, only now she could smile at the thought as she finished her coffee one Sunday morning. Now she said boldly that it was not good enough to fit in; she wanted to belong, or so she was discovering. "Whatever belonging means," she shrugged to herself. Suspending her internal conversation she went to shower and dress, and then to decide which congregation she would visit. As she left the apartment she wondered at what she was doing. Thinking of congregations to visit certainly was a change.

The intensity of this pursuit continually surprised Ashley when she considered it. But she had begun to understand it. The world in which she grew up was clearly defined by family, school, and neighborhood. Her progress through this world was easy to measure and seemed assured. The wider worlds she encountered would be faced with the same assurance, she presumed. But her presumption was wrong. The world was not what she thought, and there was more to her life than she had allowed. She could no longer fit in, because her life had changed. She could no longer fit in because she was more and life was more. But where did she truly belong? If fitting in was no longer good enough, where could she belong? Where could she be her true self in a way she had yet to discover?

We are a culture of people who've bought into the idea that if we stay busy enough, the truth of our lives won't catch up with us.

Brené Brown

Daring Greatly: How the Courage to Be Vulnerable Transforms the Way We Live, Love, Parent, and Lead

Ashley knew that she had become impatient. She was energized and she was in a hurry. She could no longer assume there were limitless opportunities and endless time. Now time was short and the stakes were higher, even as the direction she should take was uncertain. She had to do something. She had to create a new life. She had to find a place where her life could be shared and her possibilities could blossom. It was not a matter of "settling down" as her parents still intended. She had to create the right circumstances with the right people, who would understand her search and respect her for who she was. Meanwhile she felt odd and alone. She could not see that the world is full of people like her, people whose lives have changed, for whom there is no clear way to go forward. Ironically, though many like Ashley do not see it, they are not alone.

Lost in Transition

It is apparent that there are millions of young adults like Ashley who are "lost in transition." Sociologist Christian Smith has studied American young adults closely and reached troubling conclusions.[3] His particular interest is in eighteen- to twenty-three-year-olds—in other words, people at the point of transition to adulthood. Smith gives special attention to moral threads in young adult personal identity. He declares that maturity and personal well-being center on holding clear and grounded moral convictions. In a complex society people must be able to consider moral options. Decisions about moral values frame healthy relations and attune people to spiritual truths.

But the moral lives of many young adults are adrift. In some respects there are clear convictions: most young adults shun absolutism and uphold individualism. Yet most prove unable to define and defend a clear moral position. Apart from recourse to individual choice, and perceived threats to it, many have little to say. It's not that they have adopted extreme views; it's simply that they have little conviction at all. To the extent that they hold moral views, they cannot explain why they do.

More alarming, most young adults have difficulty grasping how their actions impact the lives of others or even that events may be related to actions they have taken. They may claim to resist infringing the individuality of others and take umbrage at perceived infringements of their own lives. However, they have difficulty sorting out more complex patterns of social relations, and taking responsibility for their roles in them.

Ironically, Smith finds, for an age group that staunchly defends individualism, these young adults prize their social relations. Confusion about moral values versus individual prerogative reflects their underlying intention: they are determined to gain a place in a group. Smith observes that what begins as individualism often turns on interests of social relations. The result is that one-third of the young adults surveyed reduce moral values to what others would think.[4] For young adults who seem defined by individualism, fitting in with peers is a basic drive.

One outcome of this reality is that a striking number of young adults today have no civic or charitable involvement. They do not know how to embrace a cause and to work with others to secure it. To the extent that they have political instincts, their involvement, or even interest, is momentary. They have little capacity for sustained commitment.

Likewise their social relations prove fluid and tribal. They immerse intensely in a group for a season, until circumstances, or just whim, send them in search of the next group. Such fluidity is not always of their choosing. Life transitions abound for this age group. More than simply growing up and assimilating, they have seen wars and economic downturn, and family upheaval due to job loss and divorce. With unprecedented mobility they have found electronic avenues and amusements of dizzying sorts. The result is that questions of moral formation and of being personally and socially grounded are going unanswered.

Yet somehow, sorting out one's beliefs, securing individual prerogative, and finding the right social nexus have become life's tasks for this age group. The pursuit of one's self always occurs in relation to others, even if tentatively. But which others? Which pursuits? The means of connecting to other people have multiplied. Adults of all ages now flock to social media where their whims find graphic display. How many "friends" can one amass? What late breaking news can one describe? How much far-flung approval can one gain? Draped in individualism, social media embody the pursuit of fitting in, of being appealing to others. For a moment it satisfies; then it is gone and the hunt for the next dramatic tidbit begins. Fitting in does not last.

The ambiguity of this pursuit does not satisfy all. A minority of young adults opt for rigid, authoritarian religious and political systems, Smith finds. The postmodern celebration of uncertainty, whim, subjectivity, self-construction, and fluidity frustrates some. In the midst of this social haze, leaders promising assurance become appealing to some. With unprecedented opportunities for individual choice, some opt for regimentation, even tight structure and restrictive lifestyles. This need accounts for the rise of religious groups more exclusivist in worldview and restrictive in what one may believe and do. Such ideas exert little abstract appeal. The lure is an image of a clear path to a genuine personal life in a demarcated set of relations to others. A reward and punishment system in isolation from the rest of the world gives personal benchmarks and a sense of transcending worldly confusions.

Though a minority may find appeal in such rigid religious structures, the impulse that draws people to them is broadly shared. Despite the seeming triumph of individualism, self-expression, and fluid values and commitments, there is a deeper urge. Ironically, individual acting out becomes a contemporary pursuit of fitting in, of gaining attention and approval of others, if only briefly.

Testing the Boundaries

What "fitting in" meant for Ashley's parents and grandparents has decidedly changed. For her grandparents, "fitting in" as we now see it, was presumed. You were born, grew up, educated, married, matured, and died in defined circumstances. If you moved, it was for education or military service, or work. In any case, the intention was to return "home" as soon as possible. To be sure, there have been periods of mass migration in American history, especially of people moving westward or to large urban areas. At times large numbers of Americans have sought fresh possibility; however, they did not intend that their lives would remain unsettled. Once a satisfactory situation was found, and it was pursued intensely, most Americans of prior generations gladly relinquished the idea of moving and turned to the task of fitting in.

Prior generations sought steady, lifelong employment in the same company or profession, a familiar neighborhood and friends, and memberships in local religious and civic groups. Fitting in meant the maintenance of a recognizable, orderly local world. They had tasted the wider world, and retained interest in it. But their local context, likely the one into which they were born, retained their loyalty. Family and friends were defined by it. Stable social relations mattered most.

This generation had children who tested the boundaries of fitting in. They became the generation of Ashley's parents and they were inclined to challenge the settled social worlds they inherited. For varied reasons they concluded that America and its role in the world were misdirected and they set out to make corrections. Causes defined these "baby boomers": civil rights became the paradigm. Then protests against the Vietnam War and for women's equality followed. For some of this generation, the result was that the nation went afield; for others, the nation did not go far enough. An intense "culture war" flared and its brushfires continue. The focus was social; the tasks were political. America was proving to be more diverse than most had imagined, but a powerful consensus emerged: there had to be a place at the table for everyone.

Though circumstances were broader and more fluid than in the previous generation, Ashley's parents and their generation still aspired to fit in. Their assumption about social justice was that it entailed equal opportunity to fit in for all. This pursuit was driven by an emphasis on individual rights to be sure, but recognition by society was still a goal. Eventually most of the "baby boomers" went home to jobs and families. But they made their mark. To be accepted for who one is became a fulfillment of the American dream. To a significant degree, Americans could look back on the second half of the twentieth century with feelings of accomplishment. The nation had changed. But much remained unresolved.

Even as epic struggles brought beneficial changes, disenchantment increased. There had always been American undercurrents of alienation and disaffection. The "beat generation" of the 1950s defied social norms of fitting in and cast an alternative social world. It was disengaged and sullen. Literary and artistic circles picked up the theme to a degree. As most Americans fit into jobs, neighborhoods, and families, some roamed mentally if not physically.

As protest movements galvanized, the impulse to drop out widened. In the 1960s and 1970s "turn on, tune in, and drop out" became a movement of sorts. The phrase was promoted by academic turned drug culture advocate Timothy Leary. Reflecting the idyllic innocence of the moment, Leary maintained that psychedelic drug usage would detach people from destructive social convention and bring needed cultural change. Personal freedom meant discovery of the various levels of consciousness within one's self. Drugs were thought to reduce inhibitions and release the true self. In turn, one could discover self-reliance and the capacity to choose one's destiny apart from authority figures and institutions. The naiveté was alarming.

Unfortunately, widespread drug usage became a continuing fact of American life. A linkage between personal freedom and disdain for perceived norms had been secured. The rejection of one form of fitting in had been replaced by a far more destructive form. Sadly this impulse also has persisted. The legacy of the past half century of American life is littered with groups and cults that promised freedom and imposed destructive conformity—from Jim Jones's formation of the Peoples Temple to the Branch Davidians in Waco, Texas.

Fortunately, this destructive legacy has influenced the lives of only a few. But two lessons can be learned from it: first, this legacy illustrates the extent to which people will sacrifice their freedom and individuality in order to fit in, to be acceptable to a group; second, such groups reveal the desperate spiritual search on which many Americans have embarked. Ashley is not alone, although she and her generation feel so acutely. They face agonizing, spiritual uncertainty. Opting for fitting in can be a powerful temptation; but many of them resist it.

> People are not primarily looking to cooperate with our plan for their lives.
>
> Joseph Myers
>
> *Organic Community: Creating a Place Where People Naturally Connect*

Suspended in Spiritual Space

In a New England church one afternoon three women met with the minister to plan their father's funeral. He had lived a long and fulfilling life. The family was a mainstay of the town, though the daughters had moved away decades ago. There had been nominal church membership with sporadic attendance and infrequent financial gifts by the father and mother. The family was known and liked, so the daughters were welcomed back with presumed familiarity.

However it soon became clear that no familiarity with the church, or Christianity, or any religion could be presumed. The minister's efforts to discuss an appropriate funeral service met with blank stares. Finally, trying to find the most basic starting point, he opened a Bible to an arbitrary page, handed it to one of the sisters, and asked: "Do you have a favorite passage?"

Twitching nervously, one of the sisters finally spoke: "What book is this?" she asked. Another sister picked up the thread: "Why are little numbers printed across these pages?" she wondered. The third sister remained silent and stared at the floor.

These women were neither hostile to religion and the church, nor conversant with them. Religious matters, and even less church ones, had played no part in their lives since early childhood. The nominal ties of their parents vanished when they became teenagers. The result was that their lives bore no religious imprint other than a vague sense of legacy. This shred of a link drew them back when their father died. But they were at a loss to understand what they were experiencing and how it could be grasped religiously. Clearly they had not seen a Bible in years.

It has become common wisdom, especially among religious leaders, that faith and faith communities are under assault from various directions at once. The most apparent challenge comes from within religious life itself. "Fundamentalism" has become a commonly used reference for a certain strand of Christianity. Similar inclinations can also be found among Hindus, Jews, and Muslims. Highly mobilized groups in all of these faiths, following a similar pattern, perceive that official faith leaders are compromising essential beliefs and practices out of laxity or a vain hope of social relevance. Fundamentalist movements impose rigid doctrines and puritanical ethical codes. In some cases their hostility to those outside their fold erupts in violence. They are inclined to feel dishonored and to seek redress. They can generate intense commitment among a devoted few; but their extremism limits their appeal. Nevertheless they can inject themselves forcefully into social contexts and confuse public perception of a particular religion's true nature and intention.

Fundamentalists intent on dominating religious life are only one form of contemporary challenge. Less discussed but well noted, there has been a cluster of assertive writers determined to challenge all religions. These new atheists have generally confronted religion along two intellectual avenues. Some seek to undermine religion's truth claims on the basis of science. Neuroscience has been a favored platform with special interest in demonstrating that no religious basis is necessary for human beings to learn and follow moral principles. A more practical effort to make the same point takes a simple tack: some atheists argue that religion consistently fails in practice to uphold the moral ideals it claims to embody. Religion fails, these atheists hold, because it consistently contradicts itself.

In the public eye the atheist challenge is growing almost as steadily as the fundamentalist one. Both represent threats to the historic faiths and their largely moderate followings. Yet the reality of such menaces is not easy to gauge. Fundamentalism is especially elusive. Clearly there are various conservative religious groups, some of which have taken vigorous stands on social issues. Some loudly announce their fundamentalism as a mark of pride. At times they have exerted political influence, though not often decisively. Their influence has been more to fan the flames of debate on such issues as abortion and homosexuality. There are no signs of a lasting swing in their direction, despite their capacity to promote their views.

Atheists exert far less influence and are barely growing if at all, with the percentage of those who describe themselves as such only inching upward in more than a decade.[5] Religious skepticism is something of an American tradition that waxes and wanes modestly from era to era. It also generates more social and intellectual smoke than fire. The result is that fundamentalism and atheism hardly threaten religion despite the force of public perceptions. These polar opposite stances must be kept in proper perspective.

If there is a threat to religious life now, it is represented by the three sisters meeting with a minister in the New England church. They don't oppose religion, nor do they intend to change it; rather, they simply ignore it. This thought might be puzzling to them, and the thought they were part of an emerging social trend might strain their credulity. In fact, over the past decade the fastest growing segment of American religious life has been the "Nones," that is, persons who hold no religious commitment. From just 2008 to 2012, the percentage of the American population with no religious affiliation increased from 15 to nearly 20 percent, and nearly 6 percent of the U.S. public is now self-described agnostics or atheists.[6] A study released early in 2013 noted that the growth rate of this group slowed in 2012. But the figure remains high and seemingly continues to grow.

These categories have arisen from inconsequential a generation ago to marking a major shift now. Also notable, more young adults claim these categories than older age groupings. One could argue that a historic trend toward lack of religious commitment is unfolding. At first glance such data resonate with Christian Smith's study of young adult moral confusion. By whatever means, there is a growing segment of the American population that has no religious inclination.

But firm conclusions about what this data means should not be drawn quickly. For one thing, other surveys suggest that the percentage of Americans who affirm belief in God, or a higher power of some sort, has not dropped appreciably. One corollary of the recent surveys is that well over 90 percent of all Americans believe in God or a higher power.[7] Even more intriguing are survey results revealing how people think of themselves in religious terms. Over a decade ago interest in "spirituality" surged as more Americans embraced spiritual ideals as opposed to what they saw as religious dogma. For a time "religion" lost appeal because it became linked in the public mind to authoritarian systems and to moral hypocrisies.

Over the past decade, however, there has been a shift: approximately half of all Americans now call themselves "spiritual and religious." Fewer construe being religious and being spiritual as contradictory. "Spirituality" continues to gain broad appeal and "religion" now bespeaks for many the allure of faith community and faith tradition more than older images of legalistic restrictions.[8]

> We did not leave the Church, but rather, the Church left us.
>
> Andrew Sullivan
>
> "The Lost Catholic Church," *The Daily Dish*

Such a turn is not being reflected in affiliation with religious organizations. Membership in virtually all religions continues to drop. Evangelical Christians once presumed dramatic growth but can do so no more. Even the Southern

Baptist Convention, America's largest evangelical denomination, has seen its membership drop slightly in recent years. Similarly, the numbers of Roman Catholics in the United States has basically plateaued.[9] Cynics could argue that the net effect is a decline in Catholic membership because rapid Hispanic immigration has bolstered numbers. Of course the historic mainstream denominations—such as Presbyterians, Methodists, Episcopalians, and Lutherans—have all suffered significant membership losses over the past generation, and there are no signs of reversing this trend. Mainstream institutional decline has become something of a presumed reality which leaders are inclined to ignore or to explain away.

Paradoxically, congregations of all sorts can cite growth or at least an upsurge in activity. A study by sociologist Robert Wuthnow of Princeton has described how American congregations generally take more and better outreach initiative than ever, including notable international relief and mission efforts that are not reliant upon regional or national denominational headquarters. It is notable that as religion appears to decline, at least in its historic institutional form, "faith-based organizations" have gained public recognition. It is also notable that a majority of the "Nones" express interest in congregations because of their capacity to care for people in need. There is indeed a profound legacy of compassion in the faith traditions. We will have more to say about this legacy shortly.

"Nones" or "Maybes"?

But how can some congregations grow while many others stagnate, and while membership in denominations declines? What is the answer that resolves this paradox? The religious landscape is divided into contrasting realities: the decline of historic institutional structures and the rise of creative initiative at the grassroots. In this situation, persons who call themselves

"None" can find local possibilities for spiritual growth and affiliation. One survey doubts that a majority of the "Nones" are engaged in spiritual searches or would be interested in affiliating with a congregation under any circumstances. But the Canadian sociologist Reginald Bibby has found that many persons who say they have no religious affiliation are not firmly locked into that position.[10] In other words, under the right circumstances they could find much to inform their searches in congregations. In other words, the "Nones" could be "Maybes." Recent assessments of the "Nones" reveal that over 20 percent say they pray daily, and over half say they seek spiritual meaning of some sort, many in nature.[11] The jury is still out on the outcome of their searches.

They have not firmly disassociated from religious life. Like Ashley, they are apt to test the religious water on their own terms in local contexts. Many will say, or move toward saying, as Diana Butler Bass has observed, that they are both spiritual and religious.[12] Suspicious of religious institutions, they are drawn to the thought of ancient wisdom and ancient tradition. They are also drawn to leaders and religious communities whose lives suggest that ancient ideals are being embodied today and where they find an invitation to join in this pursuit. Seeking the embodiment of faith is central for Ashley and her peers. Open doors to welcome them are crucial.

> People look for place before purpose.
>
> **Joseph Myers**
>
> *Organic Community: Creating a Place Where People Naturally Connect*

The "Nones" may pay attention to religious life as they discover that they cannot find truth, much less community, alone. Hesitant because of the images they carry of rigid systems, and the experiences that they may have had of them, they are newly attracted to testing local religious waters. They see their futures linked to the discovery of larger truth and community. They need to get over the hurdle of being introduced and welcomed to a congregation. Still wary, they are ready to discover what it means to belong.

One of the challenges in providing space for "Nones" within our congregations is that we cannot presume even a rudimentary acquaintance with faith or a positive disposition toward the sources of our faith, such as the Bible. Therefore, the framework we use to explain faith and the sources we use to support Christian values are viewed with many questions.

As a way to address this, one of our churches, which has many "Nones in search of something," recently launched "The Bible Challenge," a program many Episcopal Churches have used to read through the Bible in a year. What we quickly learned is that for this to be successful with those on the margins of the church, and even within its center, there must be the space and freedom for people to reflect honestly about what they are encountering. We cannot presume that people will find God in the text or anything sacred about it, nor can we subtly imply they should.

What we've found is that people need space to question, doubt, and even dismiss what they read. We realized that we had forgotten, if we ever knew, what it is like to try and see the sacred in shady biblical characters who are somehow doing God's will. Or how a prolonged narrative about God's "chosen people" displacing indigenous populations can be an inspiring story of faith. For many of us, our enculturation into the faith has created an interpretative autopilot that can quickly cull out the sacred. But those on the margins of the church cannot do this.

Opening the church to those outside it is messy business that leads to untidy conversations, but it symbolizes something important about belonging. We've found through this program, and others like this, that if we are a place where there can be open and honest conversations about what people really think and feel, even if it's not the accepted position, then it may be a place where they can belong.

Exploring How to Belong

To put this quest in perspective, it is important to recall that for a generation there has been discussion of "spiritual seekers" in American life. The term has been used so often it has become unremarkable. Seekers are a given on the religious landscape and many congregations have built strategies for incorporating them and their searches. In some sense, American young adults have often been seekers. But with Ashley's generation a decided change is apparent.

Her grandparents focused on life transitions and finding a settled life that defined them. Her parents pursued specific changes in the world in order to settle down in a similar way. Now there are indications that a significant proportion of Ashley's peers are neither settling down nor intent on changing the world. Ashley and many of her peers define their lives as journeys of discovery. They are determined to find themselves and to build relations with one another in new, substantive ways. They want to find truth, not be told it. They want to build community, not be given it. They are focused less on social change and more on rebuilding themselves and their interpersonal relations. They presume this will be a lifelong pursuit and that life will continue to be dynamic in this way.

The result is not that they are dropping out of society; rather they are inclined to maintain sufficient social participation to sustain themselves, and perhaps even thrive. Meanwhile there is a deep, intensely personal quest that continues. The ideal driving this quest is the pursuit of what is "authentic." Ashley and her peers intend to be authentic and to be with one another in authentic ways. They are living their lives on distinct and not always intersecting tracks: the one practical and immediate, the other ideal and long-term. The success of their journey will be the blending of the two tracks, and this is their intense goal. They hope to blend work and daily life with ideals of the self and relationship they are cultivating. They are flexible in terms of where they live: wherever they might approach such integration of their scattered selves. But the search for such integration of one's life is a lengthy one.

Ashley and her generation are in the midst of an extended liminal phase of their lives. Anthropologists speak of liminality as a period of transition. Usually the liminal period is a clearly defined transition, with a specific beginning and a clear goal marked by a straight path. The pledge in a sorority or fraternity is in a liminal phase. The recruit in military boot camp or the firefighter-to-be in training or the participant in any orientation program is in a liminal state. They are neither the persons they were previously, nor the persons they are intent on becoming. But their transition begins at a precise point, has a defined duration, and ends at a specific goal. Ashley's grandparents presumed such experiences, as did her parents in a more fluid way.

In a sense Ashley's generation is in a prolonged liminal state. They pursue life-changing discoveries, knowing they will arrive at a different place from where they started. Although their journeys have a defined goal, they are vaguely construed transitions. "Authenticity" is an ideal of uncertain dimensions. In addition their paths to authenticity are uncertain. Even the starting point, a general sense of discontent and a lack of personal clarity, cannot be defined clearly. As Christian Smith pointed out, a dynamic sense of subjectivity, of focus on one's self in relation to others, absorbs this generation.[13] Their liminal period is unclear. Their journeys are as open as they are avid. They are willing to explore and to risk. But what they will find and how is uncertain. They believe they will know it when they see it. Meanwhile they intend to enjoy the pursuit.

A key sign of being in a liminal phase is a strong capacity to identify fellow travelers and to build intense ties to them, if only for a brief period. Liminality is often linked to *communitas,* an uncanny ability to build connections not meant to endure but to inform the journey. Such ties are different from social roots. They are as episodic as they are intense. Social media exemplify this style of contact. Thus, in her book *Alone Together,* Sherry Turkle describes how technology now drives many young adult relations.[14] Electronic connections have come to reflect *communitas,* a deeply revealing but brief connection between people that is ever changing. By such ties, there is a powerful capacity now to ground community in shared exploration and discovery, even if it is quickly replaced by the next experience.

But Turkle is struck by the fact that electronic connections are proving to be substitutes for face-to-face contact. Worse, electronic encounters allow many people to feel that they can create their own reality. Loneliness can be overcome in simple bursts of contact that can be contoured to reduce complexities. Fantasy can be encouraged; reality can be filtered if it proves disconcerting. Turkle finds the worst instances involve robotic toys. Electronic pets can convey the image of companionship without dying or running away. As a result she fears that more people are desensitized to what is real. They are incapable of facing and making difficult choices, especially ones where personal values must be consulted. The line between the real and the virtual is being blurred, leaving many people emotionally stranded.

Ashley functions well in the electronic world. Her daily series of text messages to friends, the volume of e-mail she reviews, and her capacity to find information online or store her own data in a cloud all testify to her comfort. But this is information exchange, she has realized. By a fortunate instinct, she has grasped the pitfalls of posting too much information on social media. By a similar instinct she has sensed what to say, and what not to say, even to a close friend by a text. She had seen many messages forwarded too widely. She has become cautious about expressing her most private thoughts and wonderings. She liked the ability to find someone quickly. But she was hesitant to say too much.

Because they are fleeting, electronic links prove incomplete for many people, including Ashley. Out of her dissatisfaction with fleeting encounters, she began a pursuit of personal truth and ties that last. In this way religious tradition can loom as guideposts to finding oneself and authentic community. In this way Ashley and others might be spiritual and religious. They are awakening to the idea of sustained belief and community. As Smith found in his research, they are realizing that they have difficulty making choices, and need grounding as they face moral decisions.[15] The reality that they are aging, that some options have been foreclosed, and that their lives have been made worse by prior decisions, alert them to the need for a place and a framework of decision-making. Thus the stakes are high. How can they find authentic life and community? What would give their lives a lasting center of gravity?

It is clear that Ashley does not want to "fit in" as her grandparents and parents intended for themselves. Partly because of the upheavals she has experienced, and partly because she left home psychologically for good, Ashley is intent on discovering her own authentic self and on building authentic relationships. She does not want to live a monochromatic life that reflects the expectations of a previous generation. Instead, she is intent on weighing various options, judging them by what is new and different, what she can learn, and what allows her to retain creative spontaneity in her life. She had already concluded that "fitting in" seemed an abandonment of herself and of the discoveries about life she had already made.

But if she knew clearly what she was leaving behind, toward what goal was she headed? Visits to congregations arose out of a fateful realization: she needed to belong. Fleeting and often superficial ties to other people were no longer enough. There had to be a place and a group of people interested in building the sort of life she hoped to build. Part of Ashley's dilemma was her uncertainty about what this actually meant. By now she acknowledged to herself that this was a journey and she had only found part of what she needed. One thing she knew with certainty: she had to overcome the feeling of being alone, and she had to build connections to people that would extend her search and would also prove lasting.

Ashley wanted to be known for who she was. She wanted to move beyond the crossroads where she was beginning to feel stuck. She wanted to commit herself to something larger that would make a difference. She knew she could not do this by herself. She needed to find the place where she could be accepted for who she was. Although there were lots of people around her, in the apartment building and on the streets, she felt little sense of connection. Somehow she had to connect to other people with whom she could share the journey toward purposeful, substantive life. It was not good enough to be alone together. It was not good enough to try to recapture her adolescent and college styles. She had to go forward in life. But what did that mean?

If one realization had proved frustrating, it was this: she felt stuck. She had a difficult time making choices and resisted sticking with them and with the commitments to people and to projects and ideas these decisions could imply. Ashley could not decide what she really believed, to what or to whom she was committed. Nor could she envision how she would ever decide. One thing had become certain: she could not decide alone. A big part of her dilemma was simply learning how to grasp truth and how to make life-giving choices on that basis.

No Returning Home

She had grasped that life is finite. It was no longer an infinite series of disparate, self-energizing experiences in an ageless universe. So then, where was she going and how would she know when she got there? There was no thought of "going home," as previous generations would have thought. There was no longer any consideration of fitting in, of somehow recapturing a time and people and place that once existed. Such a thought was a bad joke. She was beyond returning and trying to fit in. She had to find her true, authentic self in the company of others.

Belonging had become an ideal and she was trying to sort out what it meant, and if it could be found. She assumed that belonging meant being with people who were living in authentic ways, addressing substantive life issues openly and innovatively. She had begun to think that "tradition," whatever that meant, might offer some lessons, if it could be sifted openly. In such a situation, perhaps, she could find answers for the way of life she now knew she needed.

She was admitting to herself, painfully, that she had never truly belonged. Her deepest fear was that she never would, and that nothing would make sense or matter. Ultimately, she was afraid that she might not matter. Her search for meaning had become profound, which should not be surprising. As David Brooks observed in *The Social Animal*, human beings must live in close relation to each other to extend our personal development.[16] It is how we learn values; what we learn is filtered through relations to others and to circumstances. But what relations do we build? What values do we learn as a result?

Honest spiritual seekers such as Ashley pursue this exact question. They seek to begin something true and purposeful, not to preserve someone else's creation. They seek not just allegiance but initiative. They envision truth as dynamic, open-ended, to be discovered. Yet they want something worthwhile to last, and they want to be a part of it. They also need a place to convene, a center of sorts, around which they can orbit, even if they do not always intersect it.

They wonder what it means, in the words of one author, to "flourish."[17] They sense it is a rhythm of life, and a pattern that has escaped them to a significant degree. They are finding that it means being engaged with others. Though anxious about the idea, they admit it revolves around trust. They are not clear about who and what they trust, but they want to find out. Can they discover what they seek in a congregation? At first glance the answer to this question is not encouraging.

....

CHAPTER TWO

Disconnections

Putting Humpty Dumpty Back Together

Surely congregations would readily see the spiritual struggle of Ashley's generation. Surely there are many congregations that are poised to welcome her and others who share her search for clarity and assurance. That search has brought them to the brink of exploring faith traditions and the congregations where traditions are lived. It is not hard to imagine a warm welcome and resources readily available to nurture the possibility of faith. Many congregations depict themselves as welcoming and as lively centers of growth in faith and community.

But, like Ashley, a man named Ralph was puzzled and disappointed when he visited a congregation. It was a new congregation located by its denomination on a major highway in a rapidly growing suburb. Ralph visited one Sunday and at first felt he had found a spiritual home. Finding a large parking lot that was easily accessible, he was greeted warmly at the door and saw chairs arranged in large circles around an altar. The worship was traditional with contemporary music, the words flashed on screens around the sanctuary. The sermon was clear and practical. The various announcements spoke of a lively, engaged congregation. Ralph felt his excitement growing; it felt like a place where he could belong.

Then a curious thing happened. At the coffee hour following worship, he tried to gain further information about the congregation but without success. Everyone he approached passed him on to someone else. Finally, in frustration with these cold shoulders, he left, resolving never to return. "It was strange," he later recalled. "It was very friendly for a while. But it was like being a guest in someone else's home. After a while you got the feeling that you had been there long enough and now you were expected to leave. They obviously were close to one another and to their faith; they just didn't want to share what they had."

Many congregations have "welcome" prominently displayed on message boards. But what does "welcome" actually mean in the way congregations act? Do congregations actually welcome new people, people who are different, and people on diverse spiritual journeys? Many congregations speak the language of spirituality and the spiritual journey. And many sense there is a new generation and new social realities in their midst. But all too often congregations want people to *fit it*, not actually to *belong*, especially if they appear to be new and different. That is, congregations find it easier to have people adapt to the familiar priorities and practices within the congregation. True belonging would entail changing the ways congregations set priorities and organize their activities. Quietly unwilling to do so, many congregations treat new people as temporary guests, who either adapt to how things are done or leave. The result is a profound disconnection between congregations and the realities of the world around them.

This disconnection may be most apparent in regard to spiritual seekers. But, as we shall describe, it can be rejection of any person who appears different, even at the congregation's door. One congregation in an urban area dared to send an interviewer into a diner to see what customers there knew about it. There was chagrin when, after several rounds of interviews, no one in the diner could say anything about this congregation—even though it was across the street from the diner!

It's not as if congregations are choosing to exclude people. By and large congregations, and the confessional traditions with which they may be affiliated, are in the midst of their own liminal states. While Ashley and other spiritual seekers need what congregations seem to offer, congregations are preoccupied. They face profound challenges and often fear they are facing them alone. For a generation there has been conflict and division, financial constraint, membership decline, and uncertainty over mission and direction. Many congregations report that they must attend to obvious challenges and simply cannot afford to do more or to launch new initiatives. Their perceived reality is that they are in survival mode.

The sad irony in this perception is that Ashley would say the same thing. She and her generation are, to a considerable extent, in a liminal state and are embarking on a quest to rebuild their lives on authentic footings. They don't simply want to survive life. They want to flourish. Many leaders of congregations say something similar. But unlike churches, for Ashley the search means that old assumptions and approaches have proven to be dead-ends. There is a sense of creating a new religious and spiritual self. Ashley seeks a way to belong.

Meanwhile many congregations proclaim that they are embracing "change," "diversity," and "mission"—words that would seem to position them for embracing Ashley. They would seem poised to guide and to be guided by her. But actually many congregations are trying to recreate images of clarity and purpose from past eras. They are trying to put Humpty Dumpty back together. That is, while sounding attuned to contemporary spiritual realities, they are simply trying to do familiar things with a contemporary cloak, convinced that somehow this approach will make a difference. While speaking generally about "leadership," for example, they are actually intent on more effective "management." In many congregations there are few truly new initiatives, and even fewer that would welcome Ashley. Instead there are a variety of efforts that try to do better what has already been done for decades.

It's Hard to Let Go

Thus the survival quests on which many congregations have embarked do not position them to welcome Ashley or Ralph. As both of them found, many congregations smile warmly then talk past them. They appear on each other's radar, then pass like ships in the night. But how could this be? What accounts for the failure of congregations to grasp this opportunity in their midst? Why are congregations intent on retrieving lost worlds? How might they pay closer attention to what God's Spirit likely is doing in their midst? How might they respond?

An unhelpful obsession with the past is all too apparent. In one congregation the minister energetically described how things had long been done, and still were. But it was not clear for whom various programs existed. "We have our own ways," she declared. It was indeed impressive to see hallways lined with portraits and photographs of leaders and events from as long as sixty years previously. But there was no apparent image of the congregation's present, and none of its neighborhood. It was clear there was a proud sense of legacy to be sustained. But what did this have to do with the world around the congregation? The minister paused: "Actually most of our members drive here for Sunday worship," she admitted. Few members now lived nearby and there was little contact with the realities within walking distance.

What responsibilities does a congregation hold to its past, to those who once were its leaders and to the activities and styles they fostered? For many congregations, pressed by harsh realities such as finances and division, there is enough to face. Recalling the past would seem to be the obvious path. If it worked then, with concentrated effort it can work again— or so it is believed.

But when the past is considered carefully, two things become clear. First, it cannot be retrieved or revived. Too many churches are keeping their programs on life support so that one day they can be revived. What they don't realize is that the programs were pronounced dead long ago.

> The first step in a growth policy is not to decide where and how to grow. It is to decide what to abandon.
>
> Peter Drucker
>
> *Inside Drucker's Brain*, Jeffrey A. Krames

Second, there are still lessons to be learned from the past that can help shape the present and envision the future. For virtually every struggling congregation there was a point in the past when there was vital interchange with its neighborhood. As with any interchange, there were challenges present. Thus patterns of leadership emerged to respond to them. However, these patterns do not translate literally into the present, despite the efforts of many leaders of congregations to force such a possibility. The spirit that animated the past must inform efforts to change and adapt congregational life today. But it is impossible to recapture the past as it literally existed.

What was different about the religious past that cannot be recaptured today? If one looks back to the 1950s when membership in religious organizations peaked, the differences become clear. First, in the 1950s religion was understood in largely institutional terms. Historic confessional traditions had assumed the form of large businesses. Religious organizations operated out of headquarters buildings in major cities. They ran hospitals, schools, and even commercial enterprises. They also viewed themselves as setting standards, creating standard procedures, and providing all necessary services for their member congregations and judicatories.

Second, religion in the mid-twentieth century consisted of firm identities and limited membership options, at least compared to the early twenty-first century. The idea of someone having no religious affiliation would have been astounding. At the time, of course, over 90 percent of the population was Christian.[18] Differences among Christians loomed large, especially the distinction between Protestant and Catholic. But anti-Catholic prejudice of earlier eras had subsided and prejudice against Jews also had lessened. Evangelical Christianity seemed confined to certain regions of the country. Other religions had scant presence. The term "spiritual seeker" was unknown. The notion of "seeking," especially as a broad social movement, would have seemed bewildering.

Third, the upshot was that "fitting in" and "belonging" meant virtually the same thing. They meant "membership" in a religious organization and membership was presumed as one grew up. The various, centralized organizations paid great attention to the religious education of children. Personal development was understood religiously as well as psychologically and socially. But development in this framework entailed no journey of spiritual and religious discovery. It was assumed that religious identity of a certain sort was being passed on intact. The next generation was being equipped to take its presumed place in society and in the pew. Religion and American life were synchronized to a remarkable degree. However, ferment was forming, especially the gathering storm over civil rights for African-Americans. But until well into the 1960s, being religious meant fitting into the prevailing patterns of American life.

Certain varieties of religion meshed snugly with the prevailing social pattern of American life. For those that fit this pattern, they became known as "mainline" or "mainstream" religion and included historic Christian denominations such as Presbyterians, Congregationalists (later the United Church of Christ), Methodists, Episcopalians, Lutherans, and the Disciples of Christ. American and Southern Baptists were included as were Roman Catholics by the mid-twentieth century. Reformed and Conservative Judaism embodied the mainstream style, which meant that they welcomed forms of prayer on public occasions. They identified civic with religious values, and presumed their faith should support public life. Belonging religiously and contributing publicly were synonymous.

This meshing of religious and public life provided a canopy under which mainstream religions could exist comfortably within the prevailing culture. Yet the edges of this canopy served as more of a cloak that disguised the religious and civil diversity that existed, often marginalizing those that did not fit the perceived union of religious and public life. With demographic trends toward diversity increasing, eventually the canopy could no longer hold or cloak the varied voices that sought a hearing in public life.

Viewed from the perspective of the twenty-first century, religious life of the 1950s appears to be a lost world. It was appropriate for its time, but it cannot be recaptured. Since then religious institutions have shrunk, religious options have multiplied, personal searches for truth abound. In this new religious reality, encouraging people to "fit in" according to assumptions from a different era is a futile effort. Yet this is precisely what many historic religious institutions and their affiliated congregations seek to do. Enormous energy and resources are being expended on trying to do better what has long been done. But few and scattered energies are focused on creating a community of belonging, as people like Ashley and Ralph now seek. To do this would mean allowing the Ashleys and Ralphs of the world to shape the future of our congregation, and this may be too scary a prospect for most.

> Religious systems put on people more and more pressure: give more, read more, pray more, evangelize more, attend more, learn more, try more, work more, rest more, and fail less. It's a treadmill: it's a wonder people keep coming back for more of this kind of abuse.
>
> Brian McLaren
>
> *Finding Our Way Again: The Return of the Ancient Practices*

What Emerged from the Ferment?

How did religion lose its synchronicity with the world around it, the world into which it was thoroughly immersed? While churches continue to strive to have new people "fit in," this paradigm of affiliation has lost its sway. When and how did this occur? And while congregations sense there has been a change in the religious tide, how is it that they and their wider religious traditions speak of "change" and "transformation" without considering the needs and possibilities for people like Ashley or Ralph?

We can trace decisive change to the generation of Ashley and Ralph's parents. They lived in an era that developed an acute sense of the social injustice around them and concluded that social and religious systems were flawed. They were intent on belonging to them, but they were no longer content to "fit in" as their parents had presumed. Words like "system" and "establishment" became pejorative terms that crept into the vocabulary of Ashley and Ralph's parents. People were becoming discontent and they used such terms to depict institutional and social realities they intended to change. Discrimination against persons of color was unacceptable. Injustices of all sorts were to be identified and eliminated. They were determined to change the way things were done.

Churches and synagogues were in the forefront of the civil rights movement that emerged in the late 1950s. Of course African-American churches were the foundation and the staging area. The leadership of African-American clergy, Martin Luther King Jr. in particular, was paramount. White religious leadership also joined in notable ways. Certainly some local and regional white religious leaders had misgivings, and even became vehement opponents. But the mainstream religious organizations at their national levels urged support for social justice. Indeed, social justice became a virtual purpose statement for a broad swath of American religious life, and it remains a vital reference point. From this emphasis words like "change" and "transformation" emerged and symbolized a movement that sought to make a difference by doing things differently. It was no longer acceptable to "fit in" and conform to past expectations, for one was fitting into a system that was flawed. Now there had to be change. Change became emblematic; change stamped the leadership means and ends of a generation. Its imprint remains indelible.

Not all of religious America agreed, especially as the emphasis on change broadened to focus first on the role of

women in religious life and then the acceptance of homo-
sexual persons. In the eyes of outraged individuals and conservative groups, even changes in the liturgies of some traditions
seemed designed to suit a liberal social justice agenda. This
discontent was fanned by the appearance of a few assertive
leaders and spokespersons who called for the rethinking and
revision of theology, which in turn was interpreted by some as
a rejection of historic norms of faith. The so-called "Death of
God" movement of the late 1960s, led by theologians Paul Van
Buren and Thomas J. J. Altizer, exemplified this thinking and
challenged historic assumptions about a remote, judgmental
deity and a superhuman Jesus.

Though the "Death of God" movement alarmed many
Americans, it was hardly the first instance of strong personalities challenging basic faith categories. In the 1950s and
1960s Episcopal bishop James Pike, pioneering a media presence, seemingly dismissed some faith categories, including
the trinity, in his pursuit of a contemporary way to believe.

In each of these cases, theological positions became fixed,
sides were mobilized, and a fissure between religious liberals
and conservatives hardened as varying efforts at religious
change surfaced. Then by the late 1960s the charismatic movement impacted mainstream Protestantism and Catholicism,
spilling beyond its original spiritual bounds into opposition to
the waves of change that rushed over religious life.

By the 1970s the numbers and influence for evangelical
Christianity grew rapidly. They had ready bridges between it
and the conservative resistance to the changes liberals fostered in religious as well as social life. Astonishing religious
energies surfaced and they asserted powerful social influence.
Now there were great causes around which people could rally
and dangerous enemies against which people could stand.
Various religious movements grew from this religious fervor,
such as the Moral Majority led by Jerry Falwell, Focus on the

Family led by James Dobson, the American Family Association led by Donald Wildmon, and a proliferation of nontraditional groups led by idiosyncratic leaders. The media presence of key evangelical, conservative leaders reflected the immense influence being amassed. In one case after another, groups and their leaders claimed to hold the final religious answer, the only justifiable solution to the ills of the faith community and the nation. The path to personal assurance led to affiliation with one or another group and leader.

Meanwhile the historic "mainstream" religious groups, as they had become known, suffered dramatic loss of membership and attrition of programs and institutional structures as finances dwindled. Once the backbone of American life, "mainstream" religion—Protestant, Catholic, and Jew—was hard hit by division and conflict over ends and means. Yet their response was sadly revealing more of loss than of possibility.

The instinct in one congregation or judicatory after another was a continuation of the institutional thinking of the 1950s. The past experience of synchronicity between social life and religious institutional direction left a lasting impression. The pursuit of social justice in the 1960s reinforced these assumptions. Various religious organizations followed the same course: they tried to rally fresh support with large-scale initiatives intending to address major social issues on the basis of centralized, hierarchical approaches. Enough regional leaders and responsive local clergy and laity remained to create images of a groundswell. Monies would be raised, programs would be launched, staff would be hired, purpose would be revived, and social wrongs would be made right.

In one instance after another, in the 1980s and 1990s especially, historic religious organizations thus intended to reverse their decline. In the last quarter of the twentieth century, the Episcopal Church embarked on "Venture in Mission," a major effort designed to identify new initiatives and to fund them.

The campaign faltered nationally, with fund-raising falling far short of its goal. But at local levels, talk of mission had impressive results. The campaign highlighted a widening gap between recognition of national church structures and allegiance to local congregations. During this same period the Reformed Church in America, Presbyterian Church (USA), and other mainstream denominations focused on new church development. Though these initiatives yielded results, they could not prevent overall membership loss.

Despite the best institutional efforts, the mainstream religious organizations could not swim against the tides of American life. It was increasingly clear, though not often at headquarters, that American religion had become diverse to such an unprecedented degree that old loyalties had waned and could not be retrieved, and new explorations of spirituality and faith community were redefining what it meant to belong. Fitting in by assuming membership in a religious identity one inherited was no longer good enough for an increasing swath of the population, especially in the younger generation. Now, as a young adult, one dared to go on a journey of spiritual discovery with the intention of finding authentic belonging.

> The fact that people are no longer willing to let others, including and especially the church, script their spiritual journey doesn't mean that they are unwilling to be coached. People will accept help in shaping their spiritual path.
>
> **Reggie McNeal**
>
> *Missional Renaissance: Changing the Scorecard for the Church*

The Frontline of Religious Life

Perhaps the greatest of all realities in American religious life has been overlooked amid the ferment that has surfaced: the local congregation has become central. As the identity of religious institutions has declined, congregations increasingly find that they must fend for themselves. Without a larger institutional framework, some churches are experiencing conflict over direction and identity. Others struggle as financial and social pressures descend on them, with some succumbing and closing. Amidst the decline of denominations, many other congregations have grown and still others have been born and gained momentum. In all cases, the turn to the congregation, apart from consideration of its wider religious affiliation, has become a consistent fact and a decisive change of American religious life. Congregations have always been there, but the institutional apparatus that linked and supplied them has eroded severely, leaving them as the frontline of religious life. The startling fact is that though denominational influence has waned, the local congregations' footprint in society remains incredibly large. Today, there are more congregations than any other social organization in American life.

Karen and Mark, a recently married couple in an East Coast suburb, embody both the shift in religious life and the possibility that could enhance many congregations. Karen still calls herself a spiritual seeker. She was raised in a Protestant home in the East and met Mark at college in the Midwest. He was raised as a Lutheran in a small town and knew little of other religious identities as he grew up. During their college years, later when they lived together, and after they were first married, joining a congregation was not a priority, not even much of a thought. At first they moved frequently and liked to travel when time and money allowed. There were congregations near their apartment building in the city, but they passed them by with barely a notice. Their lives were too fluid, their future too uncertain, and their own commitment to one another was still too new.

But job promotions and the chance to buy a suburban home changed their thinking. The idea of being rooted, having a home and a sense of place with important, longer-term connections and commitments loomed. With this new image of life, the thought of finding a congregation where they could belong suddenly appealed. They began to visit churches, and the search was guided by a quiet instinct rather than any concern about institutional affiliation. They paid little attention to their religious backgrounds. Instead, they sought new, common ground.

Karen and Mark found a congregation of an entirely different religious identity. It was one they never imagined they would join, whose religious affiliation they knew nothing about—or really cared. But the congregation welcomed them and the people seemed to live comparable lives. There were classes and discussion groups they attended and active children's programs for the family they intended to start. Meanwhile, dinners and other social activities gave them a sense of being rooted with people in a place. Friendships soon blossomed and the church became their social center. They had found people who lived nearby, people who were like them. "Fitting in" was not their aim. They had found a place where they could be honest about who they are and where they are in life, and they could belong to a community of faith together for the first time.

While public discussion of the state of religion in America continues, this quiet but decisive shift, larger than any of the media have realized, has occurred. The center of religious gravity has shifted to the local congregation. This shift should not be surprising: congregations are the places where the impact of religious controversy and religious possibility takes tangible form. For example, broad acceptance of the ordination of women clergy occurred less because of hierarchical decisions or institutional programs and more because people in the pews simply decided that it was right. And now the debate about the inclusion of LGBT persons is following the same path. In recent decades, change has grown from the grassroots, not trickled down from denominations.

Similarly there have been waves of popular, grassroots religious renewal that have bypassed bureaucratic institutional structures to enliven local congregations. While denominational headquarters have struggled in vain to regain their institutional bearings, many congregations under their nominal control have quietly charted their own courses with little regard for their hierarchies, responding to perceived trends and seeking ties and resources broadly. Local leaders have not styled themselves as rebels or even as disloyal to their denomination. It is just that they have found their official channels to be too remote, too strapped, and too preoccupied. The independence of the congregation has become a challenge for denominations. But it also represents an opportunity to grasp and respond to the realities outside our churches' doors.

The result has been that waves of renewal have swept across congregational life in recent years. In the early twenty-first century, there was widespread discussion of "emergent Christianity." A cluster of writers and a large number of local leaders have seized the idea that Christianity is being remade from the grassroots outward.

The emerging church movement is a loosely aligned conversation among Christians who seek to re-imagine the priorities, values and theology expressed by the local church as it seeks to live out its faith in postmodern society. It is an attempt to replot Christian faith on a new cultural and intellectual terrain.

Encyclopedia of Religion in America

The Church is Flat: The Relational Ecclesiology of the Emerging Church Movement, Tony Jones

This "emergence" within Christianity in North America is not without historical precedent. As many know, previous periods of religious renewal and revival have introduced great change. But it is important to note what actually changes and what does not. When periods arise in which religious life is approached anew and garners greater commitment, it strengthens the faith and life of people. However, it does not renew or revive religious institutions because religious institutions in various forms and eras have simply been efforts to preserve a particular approach to religious life at a given moment in time. When "emergence" or "renewal" occurs, the institutional framework is not equipped to address new religious realities, and hence it fades. Meanwhile, the religious life of individuals surges and persists.

Inevitably the dynamism of religious life sweeps aside institutional formulas and pretenses to authority. Phyllis Tickle, a popular author on religion and spirituality, advocates in her book *The Great Emergence: How Christianity Is Changing and Why,* that times of "emergence" occur in regular cycles over the centuries, revamping religious life by infusing fresh energies that reflect clear perceptions of truth.[19] "Emergence" has become an intention to find and embrace religious authenticity at the grassroots, especially in congregations. After all, that is where faith is actually lived, not at denominational headquarters.

While Tickle contends these times of emergence come in predictable cycles, we contend that there are features of the current religious ferment that make the present an unprecedented and unpredictable moment in religious life. Past assumptions about how one belongs to religious traditions have changed, which in turn means how one forms a vital and vibrant congregation can no longer be presumed. How can American congregations assess what has happened to religious life in terms that suggest what they must do now? Simply positing "emergence," as appealing as it can be, does not guide local religious life. In other words, how can congregations recognize people like Ashley and Ralph, or Karen and Mark, when they dare to visit, and offer them a vital way to belong?

Inertia and Preoccupation

In fairness, many congregations are preoccupied with obvious issues they cannot avoid. Financial pressures, often centering on maintaining programs and buildings, can be paramount. Resistance to any suggestion of change can be vehement. Conflict over issues of human sexuality and differences over belief and practice loom for many denominations and the congregations affiliated with them. Some religious traditions face breakaway movements and many face disaffection because of highly charged issues. As a result, weakened denominational hierarchies and strained connections to them, combined with uncertainty over a bewildering social and religious landscape, have left many congregations feeling alone.

The result is that many congregations have turned inward. In search of fresh purpose, looking for the emergence of new life, somehow congregations expend more energy internally than they do on the world outside their doors. The extent of this preoccupation becomes apparent when we consider the nature of conflict in congregations. Most conflict arises not because of differences over sexuality or other controversial topics. Most conflict in congregations centers on differences over direction, purpose, and appropriate leadership style. Many times it is over a mundane issue such as the color of the carpet or where the coffee pot should be placed. It is no longer sufficient to assume that religious identity is clear and consensus around it can readily surface. But in the absence of the world that once was, congregations must ask themselves what kind of community they are called to be and for whom they exist.

It is no longer sufficient to assume that references like "social justice," "transformation," "emergence," or "embracing diversity" can rally fresh purpose. On the surface they seem to reference a rallying point for congregational ends and means. But when pressed to define what these terms mean practically in one local context after another, many congregational leaders stumble. When asked to give a theological rationale for these priorities, the answers are vague and mixed. If pressed to describe how these ideals would address the concerns of Ashley and Ralph, or Karen and Mark, there would be an awkward silence.

We have seen that there are various disconnections across American religious life. Some are obvious: the culture wars that have spanned a generation; the breakdown of historic religious institutions; the turn to the local congregation; and the gulf between congregations and the growing number of people who claim no religious affiliation. But the greatest of all disconnections is truly paradoxical. Congregations are speaking in ways that represent paradigm shifts in ministry and would seemingly appeal to the "Nones" in their midst. But the ways in which most congregations act reflect efforts to preserve their lives in familiar form, reinforcing the patterns they pursued a generation or more ago. Even while sensing that there must be fresh intentions coupled with revised life and leadership, congregations persist in forms of life and leadership that reflect the past, not the present.

A clear sign of this is the way congregations approach outreach to the community around them. In an effort to stave off decline, churches are highlighting the necessity to look outward, yearning to reestablish themselves as a vital part of their communities. As a result, there is unprecedented local initiative to feed, tutor, and house people in need. But, as we shall explore further in chapter five, congregations are far more ready to do things *for* people than to do things *with* people. This approach to outreach reflects a past era of ministry and mission when the church viewed itself as possessing the things others need—from material assistance to scripting one's spiritual journey. But now the people it seeks to reach are less likely to demarcate the world with such stark lines. Instead they see themselves as fellow sojourners with those around them, regardless of their religious affiliation and social situation. Therefore what the church perceives as a turn outward may be seen as a more insular approach to ministry that keeps a comfortable distance with the very community it seeks to reach.

Though congregations and their leaders acknowledge that American religious life is changing drastically, they tend to act in ways that reveal preoccupation and inertia. The genuine challenges they face predispose them to try to manage better what already exists, preserving precious assumptions about themselves and their roles in their localities. They are not prone to risk changes in program and style. They are inclined to avoid the religious realities in their midst. Special programs for spiritual seekers like Ashley and Ralph would seem to be luxuries they cannot afford. Ultimately, rethinking approaches to ministry opens too uncertain a future and a potential loss of control. Familiar activities and approaches, even if ill-suited to the world around them, take precedence.

Postmodern, post-Christian, post-Protestant, and post-denominational. What do all these posts mean? That we know where we have been but have no idea where we are going!

Phyllis Tickle

Christianity for the Rest of Us, Diana Butler Bass

The Turn Inward

There are two clues to this inward turn. The first is an over-whelming emphasis on *process* rather than *results* and *impact*. Often this is because relations among parishioners and between congregational committees and programs take prece-dence over links beyond the congregation. Congregational life can be sufficiently fragile, or perceived as such, that enormous energies go into finding common theological and program-matic denominators. Simply finding and holding some mea-sure of consensus among the current congregational leaders and members becomes the preoccupation, the only end and mean.

However, the consensus that may emerge, often after painstaking meetings and endless discussions, is internally driven and a reflection of the congregation's isolation and withdrawal into itself. The extent to which congregational programs reflect realities beyond the sanctuary can be scant. For all the talk of "emergence" and becoming "missional," there can be precious little results. Talk of renewal may spark some new energies for existing programs for a season, but the emphasis will be on doing the same things better, not realigning them with current realities. Even outreach and mission programs are more often assessed in internal terms, such as number of meetings and monies spent on current programs. Congregational life becomes a programmatic merry-go-round.

One of the symptoms of this focus is that congregations become intent on making the church, as an institution, more successful. But people are not seeking ways to enhance the institutional church. They are seeking congregations that will help them, as individuals and families, flourish in faith and life.

Christ Episcopal Church in Charlotte, North Carolina, is experiencing great renewal and growth, and from our perspective, it is due in no small part to its focus on helping "each other grow into the fullness of God's wishes for us." They strive to help people address and move through all stages of life. How do they do this? By talking about the things that are important to people. Recently they had Glennon Doyle Melton speak at their church. She's gaining notoriety for "Momastary," her blog about her life. People are captivated by her journey, from a former bulimic, alcoholic, and unwed mother, to a path of healing. The response to her was great, both in numbers attending and impact. It is all because Christ Church realized that if the topics she raised were important to people, then it should be important to their church.

The second clue to the congregation's inward turn, then, is an increasing inability to deal with difference, especially difference in the world just outside the congregation's door. As we have noted, most congregations are far better at doing things for people who are different rather than with them. In part this is a way to manage the internal life of the congregation in an uncertain, fractious age. The idea of fresh initiatives in the local community, including building local coalitions with other congregations, linking to social agencies or educational institutions, gets short shrift. For example, few Christian congregations develop sustained collaboration with Muslims and Jews in their vicinity.

The result is confusion about what relation the congregation bears to the wider public, especially the wider religious public. Some congregations actually enhance the disconnections. They may place theological barriers in the way of participating with other faiths or of welcoming people with distinctive spiritual journeys. Other congregations declare their openness and their emphasis on being welcoming or diverse, but they inhibit entry into the congregation or interaction with other persons or faiths by the ways in which they act. As Ashley and Ralph discovered, even efforts to join a congregation may prove difficult, which we will explore in greater detail in chapter four. Advancement into leadership, after achieving membership, may prove to be a lengthy, arduous process.

It is clear that many congregations are apprehensive about the world they face. In response, their posture is essentially cautious, even defensive. Preoccupied with building better relations among the members they already have, they can be blind to innovative possibilities in their midst, even as they invoke all the right language in sermons and classes and newsletters. The result is a kind of spiritual inertia and preoccupation: it simply is unclear where many congregations seek to lead people or by what means, much less how they would welcome people who are different from their current membership. In a *de facto* way, they simply encourage fitting in while presuming to encourage belonging. But in ways that defy their capacity to envision and to act, authentic belonging is the goal of the current spiritual journey.

CHAPTER THREE

How Belonging Happens

Spiritual Explorers

By the time he was thirty-three, the brilliant teacher had already lived several lives. Education and then his popular lecturing career brought him wide recognition. But he remained restless within himself. Then he fathered a child out of wedlock. Confused, uncertain, he sought certainty by joining a rigorous, sectarian religious movement. Even though he had been involved in various groups before, he hoped to find a simpler, clearer, truer life in this one. But for all the rigor of the movement, and his avid adherence to it, the pursuit of spiritual assurance seemed endless and eventually futile. Something crucial was missing from his life, and the pursuit of it was proving frustrating. He could not seem to grasp what he most needed, and was acutely aware of his inability and his incompleteness. His mother and several close associates were dismayed as he reached an impasse.

What happened next has become one of Christianity's greatest stories of religious conversion. The man at an impasse found himself seated in a garden reflecting yet again on what to do. Suddenly he heard what sounded like the voice of a child saying softly: "Take and read." Looking around where he was seated, he saw a copy of the New Testament, for his mother was a Christian. He opened the text to a random passage and his eyes fell on a passage from Paul's Letter to the Romans, chapter thirteen, verses thirteen and fourteen. In part the passage read: "put on the Lord Jesus Christ, and make no provision for the flesh, to gratify its desires."

The account sounds contemporary. The references to cults and spiritual seeking, and to a child fathered out of marriage, read like a modern saga. But the story took place over 1600 hundred years ago. It happened in the Roman Empire, and the man's life spanned Rome and North Africa. The man was named Augustine and he became one of Christianity's most noted converts. Subsequently a bishop of the church, he would be one of Christianity's most prolific and decisive theologians, stamping a linkage between human frailty and sins of the flesh that has become ineradicable.

Major reformers in later centuries looked to Augustine's writings and his own experience for guidance. Perhaps because Augustine recorded the account of his conversion after the faith had become a secure part of his life, it is difficult to question the details of the experience or its outcome. Among his many writings that have survived, one book, the *Confessions*, tells the story of his spiritual search that culminated in his moment in the garden.[20]

Religious conversion, as Augustine's experience illustrates, is a crossroads moment that becomes the basis for a new kind of belonging. At the core of conversion is the sense of having tried various paths in one's life, but having little sense of wholeness. Augustine tested various philosophical and religious convictions and settings, until he was dissatisfied by all. Yet he was not closed to further possibility even as he wondered where to turn. The decisive turn was a discovery, not achieved by design or effort, but by sheer receptivity and willingness to follow where the message seemed to lead. He dared to listen to a child's voice, and by stages his life was transformed in ways he never could have anticipated or controlled.

Thus it is crucial to emphasize that the conversion Augustine experienced was not completed in an instant. The turn toward Christian conviction required refinement, including grounding in the life of faith community. Augustine was assimilated and rose quickly in the church because of his gifts and the power of his experience. He spoke with an authenticity that derived not just from the moment of conversion but from the continuing faith journey that he pursued. He did not and could not have embraced faith wholly or immediately. What can become instructive today is his willingness to listen and to pursue, which became the basis of his extraordinary life of service.

It is also crucial to note that his subsequent career was not a simple narrative of steady advancement and recognition. He encountered uncertainties and tensions. There were a variety of controversies and debates. He wrote and defended theological views that have been argued ever since, and he has been identified with an emphasis on original sin and human sexuality that has become troubling for many modern people. Meanwhile Augustine lived long enough to see the Roman Empire begin to collapse, thus sensing the end of the world and its values that had nurtured him. It is inaccurate and simplistic to say that he was successful; nor is it necessary simply to agree with his views because of the power of his personal conversion. But the authenticity of his experience created something of a paradigm for the spiritual search and for genuine Christian conversion.

Augustine's experience differed from what many people assume about religious conversion. Often, especially in American evangelical circles, conversion is thought to be instantaneous and whole, a kind of lightning strike that immediately reorients the life of the person, imparting instant clarity and direction. This idea can lead to a framework for conversion that insists one knows the exact day he or she was saved.

This view treats conversion as a brief, breakthrough moment with the person moving quickly from being a sinner to being saved, and knowing so with complete assurance. Of course, evangelicals understand that converts must live differently, must embrace the fellowship of the church, and must sustain their experience by study and service and prayer. But the conversion itself has been accomplished in an instant.

However, for most of the history of Christianity, and in other religions with similar experiences being reported, conversion has been an extended, less certain process. In some settings, such as colonial New England, the Puritans developed elaborate forms of preparation for conversion. They especially applied these measures to the young lives of their children, whom they prayed would inherit their faith and sustain their society. Later, in the early years of Methodism, John Wesley emphasized the time after conversion when there must be personal growth in holiness to confirm the validity of the experience. A noted English evangelical of the generation after Wesley, William Wilberforce, known to many through the movie *Amazing Grace*, was a layperson of the Church of England. He later reckoned that his conversion, in 1785, took most of a year. He struggled, not always happily or with certainty, to understand the new life to which he was being led. He concluded that his public service as a member of Parliament was the life to which God had appointed him. Yet he could no longer think solely in political or self-serving terms, but in moral and religious ideals above all. Thus he began to use his influence to instill morality as he viewed it into British life, epitomized by his leadership of opposition, and his eventual ending by political means, of slavery in Britain and its possessions.

Honest to God . . . and a Few Others

Modern cynics doubt the validity of instantaneous conversion promoted by mass rallies in public arenas as well as churches. To the outsider it can seem like a formulaic response to psychological pressure. The longer duration of other conversions can reflect what seems to be a more genuine search for truth. But whether a conversion occurs abruptly, or after extensive struggle, there is only one valid measure of its worth: Has the person who claims conversion approached and left the moment with genuine openness to a changed life? In other words, does the experience reflect personal authenticity?

We raise the subject of conversion because many people like Ashley are engaged in the sorts of spiritual searches that have often preceded conversion throughout the history of Christianity. Of course, conversion is a broader phenomenon even than Christianity's history. For our purposes, the point is that conversion most often has happened at times of personal search, and at points of intense frustration with the search. Conversion is the opening of an unseen door after various perceived doors, and religious and spiritual options, have failed to satisfy the person's quest for wholeness. In this sense, conversion has an important connection to the spate of spiritual exploration that is occurring.

This is not to say that we foresee an upsurge of dramatic conversion experiences because of the prevalence of personal spiritual searches. But we expect to see more people seeking and finding answers to their questions in intensely personal and unexpected ways. We also expect to find that spiritual discovery will lead individuals to find other people with whom to share their journeys.

Put another way, when conversion is genuine, it orients us toward others and prompts a new way of relating to others. As one sheds the façade of pretense, honesty with oneself and God grows. But the looming question is whether there is a community with whom one can be honest. A new community with a new pattern of participation is required for the journey to take hold over one's life. What we propose is that the movement of conversion transforms a person from one who seeks to fit in to one who intends to belong.

> Belonging can also be thought of as a longing to be. . . . It is the capacity to be present, and to discover our authenticity and whole selves.
>
> **Peter Block**
>
> *Community: The Structure of Belonging*

If we examine genuine conversion, it arises at a personal, spiritual crossroads where a person feels compelled to be open to new possibility. At such a moment the person is uniquely vulnerable, living between the missteps of the past and a yet-to-be-determined future. The only way forward is to be honest about who one is and where one has come from, which entails great risk. One must become vulnerable to seek personal authenticity in the form of spiritual truth—about God and oneself.

Conversion in a Cover-up Culture

For Brené Brown, vulnerability is a key category in the search for wholeness, or "wholeheartedness" as she terms it.

Brown does not speak of religious conversion as such; however, citing her "spiritual awakening" that occurred in 2007, she encourages readers to shed their protective psychological barriers. Brown senses a widespread pattern of resistance to being one's true self out of fear of not being good enough, that is, of not being able to fit in. People create exterior selves intended to shield the fragile interior lives that haunt them, while projecting achievement and assurance. In the end, they cover up who they are, avoiding any vulnerability, so that they fit in.[21]

Families, communities, and organizations can perpetuate a cover-up culture when "it is more important to protect the reputation of a system and those in power than it is to protect the basic human dignity of individuals or communities."[22] It forces one to avoid exposing any aspect of one's personality or past that may not meet the expectations and needs of those around them. When this occurs, Brown sees shame being used to keep people in line.

Unwittingly, congregations may produce a religious version of a cover-up culture rather than allowing people to show themselves for who they really are. This cover-up is costly in terms of the potential connection people can make with a community. The emphasis on fitting in can force compliance, but it prevents authentic connections with others and short-circuits the process of conversion. For this, gracious space must be created in which one can risk being vulnerable.

Brown sees a disconnection from oneself and disengagement from others as the price of hiding from one's vulnerability, which she depicts as the core truth of personal existence. Yet human beings are "hardwired to connect with others, it's what gives purpose and meaning to our lives, and without it there is suffering."[23] The risk and fear of emotional exposure can make vulnerability too steep a price to pay for connecting with others.

However, the choice between fitting in or belonging is unavoidable, according to Brown, because it represents the patterns of human connection. Fitting in represents becoming who you think or find you must be in order to be accepted by others. It is the true self altered, perhaps drastically, in order to match perceived expectations. The anticipated payoff is acceptance of oneself granted by external forces that seem impossible to avoid otherwise. On the other hand, belonging is the desire to be seen for who one really is and know one will be accepted. It is the yearning to be a part of something larger and the movement toward that larger reality and purpose in a way that evokes the genuine self, likely in ways that cannot be anticipated and certainly not controlled.

She declares that "connection is why we're here." When no façade proves adequate, many people become frantic with fear and pour increasing effort into living life incompletely or even as a lie. Such effort is exhausting; hints of the true self and of the depth of one's fear creep out. A moment of personal crisis is bound to occur. But the price of seeking to belong is a time of vulnerability for which no one is prepared and which may surface more fear and uncertainty than one can bear. Yet the goal of personal authenticity justifies the journey. "Authenticity is a collection of choices that we have to make every day. It's about the choice to show up and be real. The choice to be honest. The choice to let our true selves be seen."[24]

> [Outsiders] say Christians pretend to be something unreal, conveying a polished image that is not accurate.
>
> **David Kinnaman and Gabe Lyon**
>
> *Unchristian: What a New Generation Really Thinks about Christianity . . . and Why It Matters*

The classic understanding of religious conversion reflects the psychological journey Brown outlines, from fitting in with all its lack of resolution, toward belonging, where one is known and loved. It arises not as pressure to conform from without, but as the urge to be whole from within. It is an honest reckoning with one's human inability to be what one thought life should be. It is also the realization that there is power and possibility outside one's self in relation to which one can become authentic, whole.

Conversion is the eruption of possibility when all one had imagined finding proves insufficient and dries up. It is the opening of a door and the hint of a way forward where none had been apparent. Conversion in the classical sense entails a fascinating paradox: it is the discovery that through dependence upon a higher power (God), and in genuine relations to other people, one becomes both free and authentic. Personal wholeness becomes possible when there are the right sorts of ties to others.

This view counters popular assumptions and images cast by some conservative strands of Christianity that depict conversion as leading to a life that is morally restrictive and judgmental of others. Converts may be seen as intent upon forcing their experience on others as the only path to personal salvation. In other words, the result of conversion and the goal of evangelism is the quest to help others fit in with these religious expectations.

This idea reflects not only an internal attitude by those within congregations, but an opinion held by those outside the church. In David Kinnaman and Gabe Lyons's work *Unchristian: What a New Generation Really Thinks about Christianity . . . and Why It Matters*, their surveys revealed that of those who are ages sixteen to twenty-nine, a majority strongly agrees that Christianity is antihomosexual, judgmental, and hypocritical. Of that same group, only 16 percent would strongly agree that Christianity is a faith they respect or that Christians consistently show love for other people.[25] Popular assumptions held by some within Christianity have taken root and become barriers to those outside it.

More than a public relations problem for the church, these assumptions are the result of an exaggerated emphasis of a more modern take on conversion. Unless it is corrected, people will not turn to congregations as a place of belonging. Fortunately, the fact is that conversion seen across the history of religious experience takes a variety of forms and leads to a variety of outcomes, few of which are inherently restrictive or aggressive. As Brown has charted without speaking specifically in this way, conversion occurs at a crossroads in one's life. It is a movement through vulnerability to authenticity. We must recognize that though larger patterns of conversion experiences may surface, the journey to and through conversion cannot be prescribed.

One of the more impactful programs with which we are associated is the Veterans-Civilian Dialogue (VCD) initiative of Intersections International, a ministry of The Collegiate Churches of New York. It provides the space for veterans to share, rather than hide, the profound and tragic experiences they carry. These experiences are not easy to face, let alone reveal to others. But without a safe place to be vulnerable with those in society with whom they seek to rejoin life, intense isolation and disconnection results, which in turn contributes to high suicide rate among our veterans. VCD provides the space for connection. It represents the opportunity for veterans and civilians to express themselves in authentic ways and establish new, healthier patterns of connection. What is found in such an exchange is that the extreme experiences of combat intensify needs we already have as much as they create new ones. We all have a need for conversations and "conversions" that connect us with others.

The categories Brown provides help to make the point we emphasize: conversion, or any such breakthrough to personal authenticity, takes time. It entails the discovery (or simply the acknowledgement) of one's true self, and the charting of new patterns of relations with others. Call it conversion or spiritual awakening, or other, similar terms. The path to belonging, rather than simply fitting in, requires a period when one moves consciously toward authenticity. Authenticity means working to shed the facades and superficialities that served as shields, and admitting one's human vulnerability. What must follow, in the classic religious sense, is a period of "nurture," that is, of "formation" with other people in the life of faith. Belonging replaces fitting in as one embarks on a journey of spiritual discovery with others in the context of faith community. Just as the personal search of Augustine turned to a life of shaping and being shaped by faith community, so too must ours.

> The goal of the Christian spiritual journey is not to become less human and more divine; it is to become more fully human.
>
> David G. Brenner
>
> *Sacred Companions: The Gift of Spiritual Friendship & Direction*

Base Communities of Belonging

One can engage in spiritual probing while preserving a sense of anonymity, but deep spiritual exploration and belonging requires a higher degree of interpersonal presence, and an altered one. Congregations, when they engage with the world around them, can become the ideal setting in which this can happen.

One critical aspect of the spiritual journey begins in a stark discovery that each of us is an individual whose life is distinct, and often alone. It occurs when we have isolated ourselves, physically or psychologically, from others and are suffering from disconnection. The journey proceeds to the realization that we must explore bonds to other people in ways that are new and life-giving. For centuries religious traditions of all sorts have presumed to exemplify the meaning of authentic community as a means of connection. Periodically, in the midst of spiritual upheaval and renewal, people have created special forms of gathering on the periphery of formal religious organizations. For Christians, times of spiritual renewal have often prompted creation of small groups meeting regularly in the places where they live. This movement toward small groups emanates from the essence of what Christianity spirituality is. As David G. Benner describes in *Sacred Companions*, Christian spirituality "involves *working out our existence* within the context of the Christian faith and community."[26]

Based on this, small groups have become a presumed part of life in most congregations and now have a greater significance than ever. Over four hundred years ago, the early English Puritans sustained their movement of prayer and Bible study by reliance upon groups meeting in one another's homes. In the mid-seventeenth century, a spiritual renewal movement known as Pietism gained influence as the small groups it encouraged spread across Germany. Once again these groups met for prayer and Bible study, in homes as well as in congregations. Their influence was so great they became known as "little churches within the church."

Ever since, such groups have been the hallmark of the spiritual journey among Christians. The religious awakenings of the eighteenth century that gave rise to Methodism, and the nineteenth-century version that launched opposition to slavery and other social reforms, grew on the foundation of small groups meeting for prayer and Bible study. The conversion experience of John Wesley, founder of Methodism, on

May 24, 1738, at the age of thirty-four, occurred in a group meeting for Bible study in the Aldersgate section of London. On that evening, as he later recorded, Wesley felt that his "heart was strangely warmed. I felt that I did trust in Christ alone for salvation; and an assurance was given me that He had taken away *my* sins, even *mine*, and saved *me* from the law of sin and death."[27]

Since the time of Wesley, and the unanticipated resolution that his spiritual struggle found, the variety of forms of discovery and small group life have broadened. In the 1930s, for example, Twelve-Step programs, first associated with Alcoholics Anonymous, arose and eventually grew to encompass treatment of various addictive processes. As first formulated by Bill Wilson ("Bill W") and Dr. Bob Smith ("Dr. Bob"), the program speaks of twelve guiding "spiritual" principles. These principles include the convictions of gaining control over one's addiction, relying on a higher power to gain strength, making a moral inventory of one's errors, turning over one's plight to God (as one understands God), and so forth. Though outright emphasis on God has been challenged at times, and the reference to a higher power remains general, the original imprint of Christian spirituality is clear.

Alcoholics Anonymous, and the Twelve-Step program it christened, gained particular influence from Samuel Shoemaker, an Episcopal parish priest, who helped to secure the link between recovery programs and congregations. A rector in Pittsburgh and New York City, Shoemaker in fact became something of a model for reliance upon small groups in the activities of his congregations. Recovery and Twelve-Step groups often still meet in congregations, though not exclusively and usually independently of congregational oversight. The "spirituality" woven into such groups has never reflected a particular religious tradition. But the form and purpose remain conversant with religious tradition and many congregations seek to host such groups as a means of serving their own parishioners as well as the local community.

The small group movement gained further prominence in the 1980s and 90s when prominent megachurches, such as Willow Creek and Saddleback, began to adopt small groups as the way to be the church. They formed base Christian communities within larger church structures. Fuller Seminary, and church growth specialists such as Carl George, began to promote models and means to develop small groups so that congregations could be "large enough to celebrate, and small enough to care." Today, one would be hard pressed to find a church that doesn't emphasize small groups in some form.

A church must grow larger and smaller at the same time. Larger through worship and smaller through small groups.

Rick Warren

The small-group program is not an appendage; it is not a program we tacked onto an existing structure. The small group is part of our lifestyle.

Andy Stanley

The majority of churches . . . which have broken growth barrier after growth barrier are churches which have stressed home cell groups.

C. Peter Wagner

"100 Small Group and/or Cell Group Quotes" www.smallgroup churches.com/100-small-groups-andor-cell-group-quotes/

In the 1970s a relational form of introducing the Christian faith emerged in the Alpha Course. Though it has charismatic tendencies, it has now gained widespread use by Protestants and Catholics alike. The course is built around the sharing of a meal, a talk followed by small group discussion, and a weekend retreat. Getting people interacting with one another is the primary means to help people "explore the meaning of life," as the program frames it.

Small groups exist in congregations and beyond for a variety of purposes, proving as resistant to generalization as the word "spirituality." But in the life of congregations, small groups became the setting for the spiritual journey to become shared. Individuals must test their perceptions, their conclusions, and their hopes with others. They must have a mechanism for learning from the experience of others and finding reliable guidance. And most importantly, they must have a safe place in which they can risk and experiment with being vulnerable and honest with others. What we propose is that it is in small groups that one finds a base community of belonging that gives rise to the possibility of conversion and connection in significant ways.

Communities of Exploration

A small group that becomes a base community of belonging is rooted in exploration. As we saw with Augustine, if there is no room for exploration of belief, there is no conversion. And as we saw with Brown, if there is no room for exploration of self, there is no movement toward connection and belonging.

Sorting out one's situation, risking vulnerability, testing ideas, and finding appropriate ways forward takes time. It is more about the challenges and questions that people bring than it is the answers one can provide. If a group member tries to force a simple resolution or leaps prematurely into the image of a solution, he or she risks undercutting individual and group possibility. Without room for big questions and the space to explore, a small group becomes a class that seeks to disseminate information, not share and support one another on a spiritual journey. But in this time of uncertainty there is excitement because each group begins *de novo.*

Base Christian communities of belonging have an additional dimension. Its life is framed by religious tradition that explores the basic question: How do we work out our existence with the help of our community and the Christian faith? This question raises other concerns about how our lives resonate, if at all, with aspects of religious tradition; and whether we find our lives enhanced by seeing the tradition in a fresh light. In effect, groups weave two story tracks in fresh terms: the stories of group member lives and the stories that are recorded in sacred texts. It is the telling of stories, ones that represent our strength and our weakness, that becomes the bedrock of small group life. The details of these stories are combed for meaning, and two questions are ever present: What can I learn about the presence of God in our lives, and how can I act now in light of the possibility that power offers me?

> The stories that are useful and fulfilling are the ones that are metaphors, signposts, parables, and inspiration for the fullest expression of our humanity.... Creation stories, wisdom stories, sometimes personal stories that have a mythic quality, even if they come from the person sitting next to me.
>
> Peter Block
>
> *Community: The Structure of Belonging*

Personal stories and stories reflecting a faith tradition prompt exploration of shared meaning. But each person must be able to share distinct thoughts and approaches without the pressure to fit in. If this is sensed, people begin to feel that the group's aim is not to explore and be enriched, but to indoctrinate and force conformity. It is only through the freedom to share honest, divergent thoughts and stories that shared meaning is found.

To use a word that has gained significance in discussions of spirituality, small groups engage in *discernment*. Discernment is a process for sorting the meaning of a faith tradition for their lives in the context of the moment. In a small group functioning at its best, participants learn to speak and to listen in fresh ways. They learn to speak more honestly and openly about their lives. And when disagreement arises, as it eventually will, group members learn to stay at the table, to modify their assumptions and convictions, and to give ground in search of meaningful connection with one another.

Of course small groups can falter and even fracture. Meaningful connection is not always readily achieved. Personal views can be rigid. Participants can feel there are views they must defend, rather than appear to surrender them. Positions can be expressed assertively, even offensively. A small group considering sensitive issues honestly will soon encounter friction and an impasse that can threaten group life. Less frequently a difficult personality can absorb group energy and undercut the direction as well as the intended style. On occasion a skilled group facilitator must face the person whose manner proves detrimental. Fortunately such personalities do not always appear. But difficult discussions are ahead for a group that is addressing substantive issues for whom participants have a personal stake.

The small group has become such a staple of congregational life that even committees handling specific details of program life or facilities management in congregations can take this form. There may not be ready reference to spirituality or to personal experience if one is resolving matters of building maintenance, for example. But congregational meetings of all sorts are likely to begin and end with prayer, and an emphasis on discernment together may surface. Hopefully meetings of all sorts extend exploration of what it means to be a faith community for this time and in one's setting. Even if leaks in the roof or replacing a boiler are the tasks, it helps to remember why there is a roof or a boiler in the first place.

Both of us are wrestling with the implications of this in the lives of our own congregations. We are finding that it begins with a shift in understanding that it is no longer enough to belong to "the" community. People need a connection to "a" community within the congregation, i.e., a small group. This community can be the choir, committee, vestry, or service group—any group where people are gathered for any purpose within the congregation. As these groups are nurtured, they can become places where people belong.

At the same time these groups can feel like cliques to new people. Larry Osborne, author of *Sticky Church*, helps us understand that this phenomenon is "not so much a church full of cliques as it is a church full of people whose connectors are already full." Conversely, "new people, by definition, have lots of empty connectors. They usually share with other new people a very strong desire to get connected."[28]

This understanding alone doesn't solve the dilemma of churches feeling cliquish to newcomers. Therefore Osborne's church started "New Groups for New People." It brings the newcomers together because they all share one thing: a lack of shared relationships. In one of the churches that we pastored, we had the same approach but called it "New Community." It was a way to jump-start people's relational connection to the church by having small groups as part of the process into the church. This program proved to be an effective way to help newcomers take the first steps into community.

Such occasions can move people toward explorations of belonging, as Ashley and Ralph found when they visited congregations. Belonging, rather than attendance, begins in some type, official and unofficial, of a small group. Two key steps are taken as this happens: first, group members begin to forge an identity as a group. They acquire commitment to one another that taps unforeseen energy. They become loathe to miss group meetings. They begin to feel concern for each other and a sense of being invited into one another's lives. Second, individually and as a group (for group identity has become tangible by now), they invest aspects of themselves in a larger reality, the identity of the faith tradition they have probed. They acquire a vivid sense that it is theirs, that they have truly "joined" that tradition and begun to live it authentically.

Group members may still remain hesitant about religious doctrines, institutions, and authority figures, even defiantly so now that they have gained knowledge. They may still say they are more seekers than believers. But they have found the bridge to a larger body of wisdom and to a group whose path in life now approximates their own. In that sense belonging has begun. There are people and there are convictions to which they feel wed, at least for that time. But when small groups truly work, the imprint becomes indelible. The sense of belonging is never erased. It becomes a profound reference point, a beacon illuminating what it means to belong. When that evocative resonance appears, with a tradition and with one another, there is a decisive change. Perhaps for the first time, one can feel part of something as one's true self.

But is this enough? Is this the fulfillment of the tradition, or of one's movement into authentic belonging? The process is not complete until another crucial discovery is made: one cannot belong, nor can a group truly exist, for itself alone.

Something Larger

Ironically and regrettably, small groups can become victims of their own success. The very power of shared stories builds a life-giving capacity to share within this intimate circle. But the insights and capacities built within the group can find limited expression. A group that builds a bond among itself can focus its energies solely inward. Life in the group can be such a stark contrast to life beyond that the group takes on a life of its own. It can become disconnected from the world around it, even the congregation to which it nominally belongs.

The history of small groups and of reform movements that arise out of them is littered with illustrations of this tendency. Whether it is known movements like the Shakers, whose communitarianism lead to isolationist living, or the trend for small, disaffected groups within congregations to leave and start a separate church, these groups take on a life of their own. They begin to set themselves apart, perhaps creating a private language of their own, and even ideals that have no wider currency. Some groups can even grow as sectarian movements that steadily move beyond links to other persons and groups. The life that unfolds in these groups can be interpreted as superior to alternatives around them and meant only for the chosen few who have built an intense fellowship.

Fortunately most groups past and present stop far short of exclusivism and separation. But often group life can be so prized because of its genuine benefits that the group naturally turns inward and takes on a life of its own. The act of coming together in the hope of informing personal and shared purpose gains its own footing. Thus the means becomes the end. The group that was meant to shed light on life and the wider world becomes its own focus. It is not a surprising turn. People want to grasp tightly what has conveyed astonishing hope. They want it all for themselves, creating an unchanging bond.

The New Testament records such a story, known as the transfiguration. It is found in three of the Gospels, a sign of its significance (Matthew 17:1–9, Mark 9:2–8, Luke 9:28–36). In the story Jesus takes three of his disciples—Peter, James, and John—to a mountaintop where they have a vision of their leader in the company of ancient prophets and hear a voice declaring him to be God's son. The moment is so pure and compelling that Peter wants to preserve it by building houses on the mountain and staying there. When a small group catches a glimpse of truth, it wants to cling to it!

The temptation to hallow a group and its time of discovery together is ever present. Like Peter with Jesus, every group that becomes life-giving has "mountaintop" moments. Like that ancient experience, people in groups today must come down from the mountain. In that sense the moment cannot be preserved. In a more important sense, however, the experience can and must be preserved and extended. It is a turning point; it should make a difference. Group members may be reluctant to speak of "conversion" because it can still have weighty religious baggage. But they will likely speak of having grown, perhaps of being changed, even of being awakened or of discovering realities and truths of which they had been unaware. To be a base community of belonging, a yearning is fostered to seek something beyond themselves.

> Your desire to change your small group can't be greater than your desire to change within.
>
> **Andrew Mason**
>
> "100 Small Group and/or Cell Group Quotes" www.smallgroupchurches.com/100-small-groups-andor-cell-group-quotes/

To what might one awaken? How might one grow or be changed? Hopefully this happens in two ways:

1. That you can listen and speak in ways that open up common possibility as well as promote *healing* of painful experiences.

2. That you are *connected* within the group and, in a way more importantly, beyond the group.

In both categories a basic message is apparent: the experience is not meant to be confined within the group or within one's life alone. The experience is meant to be shared. Expressed in a different way, one acquires a certain kind of responsibility. Awakening or growth or change is not to be confined or kept to oneself, as one might store a rare commodity. Personal growth is not a zero-sum game, where one gains and another loses. The gain of one should be a gain for others; all should benefit.

Healing, for instance, is a much used and much misunderstood category. Healing is seen as the reversal of a destructive process and the erasure of something harmful. Above all it is often seen as a return to a prior and better state of life. It is also seen as inherently and intensely personal. Instead, in the sense in which we are speaking, healing is not a return to a prior state of life—healing is movement forward into an entirely new and more complete life. Healing in this sense does not erase the past; but the pain that arose in the past, in physical and emotional and spiritual forms, no longer controls who one is, or how one feels and acts.

The healing associated with spiritual well-being requires other people and has implications for other people. As we have urged in this chapter, and throughout this book, the healing that is part of belonging requires new patterns of reliance upon others. Similarly, when you have healed, and begun to interact with other people in fresh ways, those people benefit from the new self you present.

It has become clear from the writings of Edwin Friedman and Peter Steinke that "family systems" is a metaphor for the intense interconnections of people in social systems. Drawn from the pioneering work of Murray Bowen, Friedman and Steinke have applied family systems theory to religious life, especially to congregations. The key discovery is that people connect in varied ways, inevitably impacting each other by the patterns of behavior they evolve. The resemblances to patterns of behavior in healthy and unhealthy biological families are striking, which helps one to recognize that the bonds among people drawn together by faith journeys can be very powerful. For both these writers there is the stark reality of unhealthy patterns of connection, and they devote many pages to how skilled leaders must confront and alter destructive patterns.

It is all too common to find leaders enmeshed in unhealthy systems, struggling to find a way forward. In such environments, leadership often constitutes reacting to the emotional instability that surrounds them. In *Failure of Nerve: Leadership in the Age of the Quick Fix*, Friedman builds on previous work to argue that to effect change would-be leaders must overcome anxiety and reactivity in the systems they serve. He says that "any renaissance, anywhere, whether in a marriage or a business, depends primarily not only on new data and techniques, but on the capacity of leaders to separate themselves from the surrounding emotional climate so that they can break through the barriers that are keeping everyone from 'going the other way.'"[29] There is no quick fix. Instead they must develop stamina and a spirit of adventure so that they can effect change in unhealthy patterns in groups.

But it should not be presumed that in small groups pursuing spiritual and religious growth, or in congregations and larger religious systems, there is inherent dysfunction. The mere fact of being linked religiously or spiritually is not unhealthy; the pursuit of wholeness, and of the authentic belonging that is its outcome, must surface the personal and familial and social hurts that are part of the fabric of human life. There is no wholeness without healing, and no personal or shared authenticity without moving through and beyond what has hindered us as individuals and as communities.

Therefore it is crucial that small groups and moments of awakening point beyond themselves. One must be dubious about claims of immediate conversion and sudden, unquestioning belief. The great examples of Christian conversion surface immense struggle before and after the experience of a decisive moment.

Radical Reorientation

We mentioned the conversion experience of William Wilberforce in 1785, and his subsequent role in galvanizing opposition to slavery in Britain and its colonial territories. His life offers further instruction for us now. For one thing, the greatest outcome of Wilberforce's awakening to faith (he never seized upon the word "conversion") was a profound sense of having his life reoriented, or diminishing connections to some people and awakening connections to others. He diminished his once elaborate social life and club memberships, for example, not out of dismissing his former social circles, but out of having little further time for them. The experience of awakening conveyed a deep sense of responsibility.

Above all Wilberforce discovered a sense of connection to people in need. These were not people he had ever met, nor people he necessarily would meet. Yet in a profoundly spiritual way he felt confronted with a sense of common humanity, of every person being a child of God equally with one another. In light of that equality, the fact of slavery, and of poverty in every English community, became a divine judgment upon British presumptions. In a way that is difficult to explain without applying the lens of faith, Wilberforce felt connected and he felt that his "station in life" (social privilege) gave him a religious and moral responsibility to act in ways that tangibly bettered the circumstances of people who by sheer fate suffered because of who they were.

His life after religious conversion became a spiritual, as well as political, journey of its own. From 1785 and the period of awakening to his death in 1833, Wilberforce devoted his influence and personal resources to improving the lives of others. His signature cause was the eradication of slavery. It is noteworthy that he joined with a small group of similarly motivated persons who became known as the Clapham Sect. They bought houses in what was then the prestigious London suburb of Clapham so that they could better coordinate their common work. They became known as a sect, somewhat cynically, because the intense bond of a small group was apparent among them.

Wilberforce is not alone in the movement of his spirituality. In 1888, Vida Scudder was an academic who awakened to a commitment to religious life and social initiative. She helped to found the Society of Companions of the Holy Cross, a women's prayer and social action group. In 1890 she was the cofounder of a settlement house in Boston. These are but two examples of communities she helped form that, through their social bonds and spiritual impulse, helped improve the lives of others.

This pattern can be found in the way congregations organize themselves. The Church of the Savior in Washington, DC., organizes itself through small groups, which is nothing new. But these groups search for a shared sense of ministry in which they can positively impact the lives of others. The DNA of their groups creates a bond that points them to others.

[John] Wesley wasn't persuaded that someone had made a decision for Christ until that person became involved in a small group.

Joel Comiskey

Home Cell Group Explosion: How Your Small Group Can Grow and Multiply

These examples illustrate the lesson all small groups must learn, especially those pursuing spiritual growth and even religious awakening: what they receive cannot be hallowed and preserved as if it belongs in a museum. They have been given a gift; the gift proves stillborn unless it is shared. Spiritual growth is meant for all; it radiates outward. We can and must choose to apply our gift to the betterment of others, although we cannot control the outcome. But what we discover, and what we conclude as a result, are crucial. They can make many lives better.

CHAPTER FOUR

The Messy Business of Belief

From Truth to "Truthiness"

As they approach the Eucharist at St. Mark's, a small suburban Episcopal church, Ashley listens attentively as the priest recites the liturgy:

> Holy and gracious Father: In your infinite love you made us for yourself, and, when we had fallen into sin and become subject to evil and death, you, in your mercy, sent Jesus Christ, your only and eternal Son, to share our human nature, to live and die as one of us, to reconcile us to you, the God and Father of all. He stretched out his arms upon the cross, and offered himself, in obedience to your will, a perfect sacrifice for the whole world.

Ashley gives a slight nod in her seat, affirming the depth of what this moment means to her. After the service, Ashley waits in the "receiving line" to greet Father Jim as the congregation departs from the service. In the brief moment speaking with him, she mentions how much communion meant to her. She tells Father Jim that she has been struggling personally and spiritually, and she experienced God's love in the service.

At the vestry meeting on Monday evening, Father Jim shares how moved he was by Ashley's comments after the service. He has been telling the leadership of the church that they need to do a better job of conveying the fundamentals of the faith. Too many churches have lost their way and no longer know what they believe, and his encounter with Ashley reinforced his notion that people still need and are yearning for the truth of the gospel.

Meanwhile, on that same Monday evening, Ashley is meeting her friends for drinks, and she mentions that she attended a service at a local church yesterday. Her friends, while usually supportive of her, begin their typical rants about the latest sexual scandal with priests and how old-fashioned the church is. Finally, one of her friends turns to Ashley and asks, "Do you really believe all that stuff about Jesus being raised from the dead, and that Christianity is the only true religion? It all seems pretty far-fetched and narrow-minded." Ashley quickly replies, "I'm not sure I believe all of that. And I can't say that it is true for all people. I just know that it helps me when I struggle."

It is clear that what Father Jim proclaimed and what Ashley took home are very different from one another. A change is occurring in how people approach belief that has been so subtle that it has escaped the attention of many church leaders. While surveys show that the number of people reporting orthodox Christian beliefs has remained relatively stable, individual conversations with those who attend reveal that something quite different is emerging.

Some time ago, the sociologist Robert Wuthnow gave indications of this trend when he described this change as a shift in what people may now intend when they affirm orthodox expressions of faith. While previously a person's affirmation of beliefs meant they are true for all people, increasingly people are only giving a personal affirmation that it is "true for me." This becomes a hedged orthodoxy that allows people to affirm orthodox doctrines by placing limitations (though not always publically voiced) for whom this truth may be relevant.

Over time, pollsters have also discovered that what is "true for me" has come to include new beliefs and a rejection of a few old ones. The Barna Group, a leading evangelical research and polling organization, has found that while 38 percent of the population is self-defined as evangelical, only 8 percent have beliefs that qualify them to be categorized as evangelical.[30]

While churches continue to proclaim the Christian faith, leaders need to know that two changes are occurring for those who sit in the pews. As people affirm Christianity as "true for me," they may only be loosely embracing the tenets of Christianity. And taking this a step further, a growing number of people are attending church despite its beliefs, not because of them. What we are proclaiming and what people are taking home may not always be the same thing.

This trend toward "true for me" signals a change in how an increasing number of people are using the term "truth," if they use it at all. If someone speaks of what is "true" or is "truth" with respect to faith, it may not be that he or she is professing that the truths of Christianity represent a body of statements and propositions that are factual. And it may not have anything to do with the truth of the faith over against other faiths. When people comment on the truth of their faith, they probably mean that faith works for them. The logic is that if it works, then it is true for me. The truth of faith is less and less about being in accord with what is factual. It is about whether what a person believes helps them in addressing their needs.

Stephen Colbert popularized a new term to capture this new take on truth. He calls it "truthiness," which several years ago was named the word of the year by the American Dialect Society (ADS). Colbert says that "truthiness" is "truth that comes from the gut, not books." Therefore when someone speaks of "truthiness," it means "the quality of preferring concepts or facts one wishes to be true, rather than concepts or facts known to be true" (ADS).[31] It expresses a truth that works "for me." This term caught on quickly with the Colbert Nation, the legions of people who watch the Colbert Report. With this in mind, one could say that while church leaders are concerned with the truth of the faith, people are more interested in whether it has personal truthiness for them. This idea helps explain the gap between what church leadership proclaims and what people hear, what pastors preach and what people take home.

New ways of engaging one another about differences in our beliefs are emerging. In teaching an adult education class during Lent, a conversation emerged about the resurrection. One person shared the hope she finds in the resurrection, another denied that there was a resurrection, yet another said we should interpret it as a metaphor, and someone else concluded by saying he is uneasy with anything that is in the Bible. Not long ago, this would have presented a messy situation that the class would expect the teacher to sort out so that no one left confused. However in this group, there was no anxiety about people being all over the map with their beliefs. No one felt an impulse to sort out who was right or proclaim what was right for all. What was prized was the ability to share divergent views in the search for truthiness, not to leave with the truth.

> People are far more interested in what works than what's true. I hate to burst your bubble, but virtually nobody in your church is on a truth quest.
>
> Andy Stanley
>
> *Deep & Wide: Creating Churches Unchurched People Love to Attend*

Celebrating Heresy

Researchers have confirmed that the substance of the Christian faith is shifting. In her book *Almost Christian: What the Faith of Our Teenagers Is Telling the American Church,* Kenda Creasy Dean describes the trend in the beliefs of our youth, and this new religious outlook called Moral Therapeutic Deism. Creasy Dean delineates the five aspects of this outlook:

1. A god exists who created and orders the world and watches over life on earth.
2. God wants people to be good, nice, and fair to each other, as taught in the Bible and by most world religions.
3. The central goal of life is to be happy and to feel good about oneself.
4. God is not involved in my life except when I need God to resolve a problem.
5. Good people go to heaven when they die.[32]

The conclusion reached is not that this is an outlook that teenagers have adopted in reaction or opposition to orthodox Christian beliefs. It has been passed on to them through their churches and parents. It is all they know.

What is further disheartening is that this new outlook does not represent anything that has real relevance in their lives. In fact, teenagers struggle to articulate anything about what they believe. The lens of faith is not how they see the world. Creasy Dean sees it as an indication of a "benign whateverism." It represents a positive disposition toward religion but no commitment to it. As she puts it, "Faith, and the church that perpetuates it, are increasingly seen as nice but irrelevant to the substance of what makes a good life."

She has also found that the religious disposition of our youth lacks four theological accents that give faith its life-transforming character: "a creed to believe, a community to belong to, a call to live out, and a hope to hold onto." Without this, faith has become inconsequential and the church has been sidelined as a life-giving community to which one would desire to belong.

Many use this to take aim at the church and blame it for not fulfilling its responsibility in teaching its youth the distinctiveness of the faith and modeling what it looks like when lived. However, it raises an important question. Have our youth embraced this new outlook because it is what the church and parents have taught? Or have they embraced it because it is what they feel they can believe? If it is the former, then the solution is simple: do a better job of modeling and educating our youth in the faith. If it is the latter, then it points to a shift in how people are approaching belief itself. We believe it is the latter.

Part of the reason a growing number of people are expressing unorthodox Christian beliefs is that these ideas had previously been concealed. Until recently, kinship and community pressure had a way of suppressing people's personal beliefs and doubts while nudging them toward conformity of behavior and expression of belief. For many, being accepted in their community meant they needed to be church going, doctrine affirming, Bible believing Christians.

In our current milieu, not only is there increased space for people to express dissent and difference, some are feeling compelled to do so. Tanya Marie Luhrmann sees this as the result of our increasing awareness of the uncertainty of our knowledge, and with this the availability of disbelief. She says, "The availability of disbelief is a condition of modernity. You cannot but be aware that other people think differently—that they may disbelieve your belief."[33]

Millennials (born after 1980) and Gen Xers (born from 1965 through 1980) not only see their generations as different, they desire to be different. Why is it that nearly 40 percent of them have tattoos, relish generational monikers, and have personal websites labeling their personal identity?[34] Why are they so actively blogging, tweeting, and feverishly posting pictures on Instagram? In part because they are branding themselves as unique and different.[35] This quest to be different not only applies to hair color and body piercings, it applies to the way they are approaching belief.

One could say that this new generation not only accepts heretics, it celebrates heresy. Heresy is "dissent or deviation from a dominant theory, opinion, or practice," and with respect to the faith, it is carrying a position that is contrary to church doctrine. For many, heresy is the pathway to finding a true and authentic expression of faith. It is not that they want to disprove church doctrine, but without the space to challenge dominant assumptions and explore new positions, they feel stifled in their spiritual quest. People are not looking for a church that pressures them to fit in with what others expect of them. They desire a place where they experience the space true belonging offers so that each person has the room to approach faith in his or her own, unique way.

A long time ago, "generation" referred to fathers and sons and grandfathers. . . . . Now the word "generation" has become a metaphor, a shorthand into which we pour our identities and dreams.

Monica Hesse

The Washington Post

The ease with which people are flirting with "heresy" may make some uncomfortable. But the way they approach theology is sure to confound others—especially if one has any affinity for systematic theology. Past emphases on theology have stressed that it is not only important to know what one believes, these beliefs must also cohere as a system of belief that is orderly and rational. The end result is that our beliefs must complement and not contradict one another. A conflict in two beliefs signals a theological problem that requires a solution. Today people no longer think about beliefs in terms of *coherence*. Instead they want to know if a belief *corresponds* to what is real and true. If two beliefs conflict with one another, within a religion or between religions, there is no problem to solve because it reflects a God who is larger than any belief system. There is no a compulsion to debate which belief is true. People are ready to accept that both are true.

Church leaders now find it exceptionally difficult to know how to reach a changing culture that is rethinking religion and religious commitments. How do you connect with people who celebrate heresy and are questioning, if not critical, of what the church believes and represents in the world? And let's be clear about whom we are really speaking. Though we have cited Millenials and Gen Xers as depicting the dilemma, the issue is far greater than these two generations. These issues have been brewing for the last three centuries, and what has occurred is that the challenges are becoming more evident in the last two generations.

We recognize that this is bad news for the Millennials, who may like to see themselves as more distinct than they are, and for church leaders, who must recognize the issue is not confined to one or two generations. Thus the premise of our work is not how to cater to one or two generations. We are using them as the most vivid example of what is before us: How do we respond to a new cultural context that is enveloping all of us?

One approach is to see this as a threat and circle the wagons to protect our beliefs until people are willing to embrace faith on the church's terms. This approach, however, holds little hope for success. To do this is to ignore one's cultural context and the needs and approaches of those outside the church. History has shown that churches that are unable to relate to a new cultural context will soon find themselves disconnected and irrelevant to people's lives.

On the other hand, the solution is not to jettison any beliefs that a new generation finds questionable in the quest to attract them. This approach caters to personal preferences and offers nothing that stretches us or points us to something larger than ourselves. In the end, the message and mission soon become too small to sustain a community of faith. There is another way, and it begins by calling upon our faith heritage to help us see the role of belief and the possibilities of faith in a new light.

The Recovery of Belief

What we have described may seem to paint a hopeless picture for the recovery of belief and the continuation of our Christian heritage in our current cultural milieu. However, if we are willing to rethink past approaches, there are aspects of the Christian tradition that have been forgotten or neglected that have the potential to be catalytic in connecting the heritage of our faith with a new generation. In particular, we hold up three elements in this recovery of belief: 1) reframing what it means to "believe," 2) the sequence of belonging, believing, and beliefs, and 3) an understanding of how belief happens.

1. Reframing What It Means to "Believe"

All churches, in some form or fashion, ask every person who wishes to become a member the following, "Do you believe . . . ?"

We ask if they believe in God. We ask if they believe in Jesus Christ. We ask if they believe in God's Word. Each church has its own way of doing this, from the most liturgical to those who like to exercise a little "pastoral freestyle" in these moments. They all inquire about belief as the threshold to becoming a bona fide member of the church.

So here's a novel question. What do we mean when we say we "believe"? And more importantly, what should we mean when we say we "believe"? We use the terms "belief" and "believe" so frequently that we may never consider the answer to these questions, yet it lies at the heart of whether or not one can belong to a church. And when it comes to the problem of belief today, it is not that a new generation is turned off by belief. They are pushing back on what we mean when we use the term. Therefore it will serve us well to examine what we may be communicating in the quest for people to believe.

Probably what most of us mean when we say we "believe" is that we are giving intellectual assent to a set of propositions that summarize the things we accept as facts. It is about creeds, statements, liturgies, and the tenets of Christianity. If you assent to the beliefs of a church about God and Jesus (each denomination has its list), then you are a Christian and accepted into the community of faith. Today's youth are unwilling to sign off on this list for countless reasons, many of which we have cited earlier.

However, one of the major reasons is that this notion of belief as intellectual assent offers little hope for transformation. Our youth are savvy and know that just because we believe something to be right and true does not mean it changes us in anyway. We can believe that Christ died, Christ has risen, Christ will come again, but still live with great anxiety. We can believe that we are saved, but still experience depression while we wait in heaven's holding station, the church, for paradise to finally arrive. In all of this what is missing is a connection between what we believe and what changes us. Belief in the sense of intellectual assent is about who and what is right. But what people are seeking is something that works to change and transform us.

Fortunately, the phrases "to believe" or have "belief" have a fuller meaning that better captures our heritage and more readily resonates with our current context. Marcus Borg, drawing on the work of Wilfred Cantwell Smith, helps us understand the history of the usage of "belief" and how it has morphed into a new meaning in recent centuries.[36]

Both the Apostle's Creed and the Nicene Creed begin with the Latin word "credo," which means, "I believe" and is the root meaning of "creed." When this word was originally recited by those ready for baptism, it did not mean "I accept the following things as true and factual." It meant, "I give my heart to . . ." To express belief was not about the state of one's knowledge as much as it was an expression of trust, loyalty, and commitment to a life-changing relationship. Prior to the seventeenth century, the object of belief was a person, not doctrinal statements. Someone to be "believed" was someone to be "beloved," two terms that are related to one another.

As we think about the orientation of Jesus's life and teaching, it makes sense that this would and should be the emphasis. When Jesus was asked by a Jewish leader about which is the greatest commandment—and for this crowd, commandments really mattered!—Jesus responded with the summary of the law that we all have come to know: "'You shall love the Lord your God with all your heart, and with all your soul, and with all your mind.' This is the greatest and first commandment. And a second is like it: 'You shall love your neighbor as yourself.' On these two commandments hang all the law and prophets" (Matthew 22:37–40). Does it not then make sense that to follow the way of Jesus is more about an expression and commitment to a relationship with

God than assent to thoughts about God? This is one of the main functions the creeds served; they were a vehicle for people to express their fidelity to God through Christ and their commitment to carry on the core of Jesus's example and teaching on love and relationships.

This idea is freeing when it comes to engaging the central material source of the Christian faith, the Bible. It shifts how we see our sacred text. For many, one of the goals of the church is to help people "believe in the Bible." This may be so if belief is about intellectual assent and the facts we must affirm are in the Bible. But if belief is about giving one's heart to God, then the goal is helping people encounter and believe in God, the One to whom the Bible points. After all, people don't show up at the church's doorstep to develop a relationship with a book. They want to experience God.

How, then, do we handle the challenge of reaching a new generation? When someone visits a church, it is never done casually and entails an element of risk, which we in the church easily overlook. For those who venture into a church today, there is always the lingering thought of rejection because he or she is not like the regular churchgoing crowd in thought or behavior. So what gets someone out of bed early to go to church rather than sleep late and enjoy brunch with friends? It revolves around two things: a desire to give one's life to something larger than oneself, and a need for connection and belonging. We must recognize that the journey of faith never begins with the thought, "I think I need some new literal-factual truth in my life." It begins with a desire for a new orientation in life and a community that will support living life in a new way.

There is good news and bad news in this. First, the bad news. If the church continues to emphasize the modern meaning of belief—intellectual assent—it will only alienate those who are on a spiritual quest. The spiritual journey does not begin with a desire to know about God; people yearn to know God.

Now, the good news. People desperately want to believe. They want something and someone they can trust and give their hearts to. And through this relationship, they want to find new direction and purpose for their lives. Belief is a way forward in this quest. It is about giving one's heart to God. It is about trusting God to provide direction for the whole of our lives. The Bible, creeds, liturgies, and traditions are the instruments to help us build this trust. When we confuse these instruments as the object of our belief, we miss the mark.

Tanya Marie Luhrmann makes an interesting personal observation about belief: "We think of belief as propositional, and of faith as an attitude, an orientation, a way of committing to a sense that the world is good despite all evidence to the contrary. So from that perspective, I resonate with faith." The conclusion she reaches is this, "Belief is tough for me."[37] She represents a much larger populace who has also struggled with belief. But it is not because of what belief could mean to them; it is because of what we have made it mean for them. The church needs to reconsider what it is asking of people when they ask for them to say, "I believe . . ." The living waters of our heritage offer an old meaning that can help a new generation discover what it means to believe in God.

2. *The Sequence of Belonging, Believing, and Beliefs*

After all we have said about reframing the meaning of belief, it does not mean that there is not an element of intellectual wrestling and assent in the process of giving one's heart to God. Beliefs, as distinguished from belief, are those things that we affirm about God and are an integral part of the spiritual journey. We can think of it in this way. People who come through the church doors are definitely looking for something larger to which they can give their lives: the search for belief, i.e., something they can trust and give their hearts to. But whether there is a god or not, and if there is, what one can know and experience of God, remain questionable. Therefore in the process of learning to believe and trust in God, people are also establishing beliefs about God. Here is what is important to know about this process: unwittingly, when and how churches emphasize beliefs may be estranging people from their pews.

As we stated earlier, people are prompted to attend a church for two reasons: a desire to give oneself to something larger, and a need for connection and belonging. In church circles, we label the first pursuit as developing faith in God and the second as becoming a member of a church. We have a well-established pattern for how this works: first you sort out your God questions (do you believe in God as revealed in Christ and do you affirm what we know about God through Christ?), and then you can become a member. It may be surprising to learn that to those on the quest, this sequence feels completely backwards.

Here's why. It feels like the church is forcing you to fit in. If you affirm the things we want you to affirm and act like we expect you to act, then you can join us. Again we go back to the seminal insights on fitting in and belonging by Brené Brown: "Fitting in is about assessing a situation and becoming who you need to be in order to be accepted. Belonging, on the other hand, doesn't require us to change who we are; it requires us to be who we are."[38] To many people, the process of becoming a member is about fitting in, not belonging, and this does not work for them. Part of what they seek is a place to belong, to show up and be seen for who they really are, with all their questions and doubts, and know there is a place for them in the community. If there cannot be a place for them in the community when they are in a vulnerable place with respect to faith, how will they be treated if they reveal other vulnerable places? They are not going to stick around to find out. What they want is to belong before they believe.

In a recent new members class, one of us was asked, "I'm not sure I believe any of this stuff you talk about with Christianity, though I used to. And I'm not sure I ever will again. However, there are things I need to sort out in my life and in my faith, and this is place I want to do it. I've been attending for several years, and I love this place and want to fully be a part of it. Can I become a member?" So how would you respond?

The pastor's past training told him that there was too much for this man to sort out for him to become a member, but everything within him said that this is exactly the place this man should be. Therefore he answered, "If you are asking if we are willing to avoid the distinctiveness of the Christian tradition so you or anyone else would be more comfortable, then obviously, the answer would be that this may not be the right place for you. But I don't think that is what you are asking. I think what you're asking is if we are willing to accept you as you explore, question, and challenge the Christian faith. And when we ask the 'do you believe' questions, though you may struggle with them, if in your heart you know the key to your journey is found in them, then our answer is that this is definitely the place for you and we welcome you with open arms."

We know this may sound untidy and improper, but it is what it means to follow the way of Jesus. If Jesus had insisted that people must believe before they can belong, then the Christian movement would have died with the first disciples! We encourage you to go back and reread the Gospels with an eye toward this. Notice that throughout the Gospels the disciples vacillated in their beliefs about who Jesus was and what this meant for how they understand God. When this occurred, Jesus did not label them "in" when they seemed certain and "out" when they had questions and doubt. They were always "in" because they had committed to be in relationship with him. Through the course of this relationship, they wondered what they had gotten themselves into, even to the point of considering abandoning the journey. But as long as the thread of relationship remained, they were a part of the community of faith to which Jesus had called them.

If we are truly committed to Jesus and following the way he showed us, then we must be ready to extend the space for people to belong long before they have sorted out their beliefs. People are ready to believe (give their hearts to God) long before they can articulate their beliefs. For many, the initial impetus to belong is a desire for a relationship and connection to God and a community. They, like Jesus's disciples, want to respond to this yearning and begin the relationship with God through Christ so they can build greater understanding and trust in the beliefs that bind us in relationship with God and one another.

This reordering of believing and belonging turns the typical concepts of evangelism and membership assimilation upside down. Willow Creek Community Church and Saddleback Community Church articulated a theory of evangelism that begins with the premise that people are seekers and need a place in which they can find what they seek. In their approach, churches should be places that are "seeker-sensitive" so that people have a safe environment to sort out their beliefs. After doing so, these people move from seekers to believers who can become members of the church. However, the challenge before the church is not to end a seeker's search and eliminate their spiritual uncertainty before they can belong. The need today is to become a place where one can continue being a seeker while belonging to the community.

It is only through belonging to a Christian community that our trust grows in our relationship with God, our lives are changed, and we can better articulate the reality of God. To force people to articulate their understanding of the reality of God before belonging is often not possible, and in doing so we may force people to create the illusion that any spiritual uncertainty is gone and short-circuit the earnestness with which they can pursue their spiritual journeys.

> We cannot easily give our heart to something that our mind rejects.
>
> Marcus Borg
>
> *The Heart of Christianity*

Some may think that allowing the articulation of beliefs to come much later in the journey diminishes the value of the doctrines, creeds, and liturgies that have become our touchstones for affirming the truths of our faith. We would say that it in no way diminishes their value, but it does force us to consider the roles these may play in the journey of faith.

In George Lindbeck's influential work, *The Nature of Doctrine: Religion and Theology in a Postliberal Age*, he outlines the primary ways we have understood the role of religion and its attendant theology and doctrine.[39] One approach is to see religion as a cognitive or propositional endeavor in which religion is comprised of propositions and truth claims that one embraces. Under this understanding, we recite creeds and liturgy as a way to hold these truths before us. The second is to see religion as "experiential–expressive" in which our theology and doctrines are symbols of inner feelings and dispositions. In this approach, the development of doctrine, creeds, and liturgy arose as a way to describe what is going on within us.

Lindbeck proposed another way of understanding the role of religion and its doctrines. He calls it the "cultural-linguistic" approach.[40] Just as culture and language shape how we engage and experience the world, so too religion, with its theology, doctrines, and liturgies, shapes how we experience the world and live in it. In this sense, it "regulates" our lives and provides rules to live by. The term "rules" may sound stuffy and legalistic, but in its best sense it represents those things that have an ability to change and transform us, which hearkens back to the early understanding of the teachings of the church as *regulae fidei*, the rule of faith. These are the things that, when they become normative for us, have the ability to lead us to live transformed lives.

This concept is important for three reasons. It reminds us that it takes time to learn and assimilate beliefs into our lives; the journey to change is a lifetime pursuit; and the role of beliefs is to inform how we experience the world and help us flourish in it. We can continue holding up our beliefs as propositional statements that people must accept to belong in a church. Or we can embrace people who yearn to belong, affirm their desire to believe (give their hearts to God), and give them the time to live with the vast resources of our beliefs found in our liturgies, creeds, and doctrines. It is only through experience that we are able to embrace beliefs as a life-giving force. Churches must create the space and opportunity for people to grow into them. It is part of the journey that never ends.

3. How Belief Happens

Lindbeck's emphasis on the "cultural-linguistic" dimensions of belief also suggest how it arises. Belief cannot be passive, rational assent to abstract formulations. Belief arises through participation in the nonverbal and aesthetic aspects of faith community. We recalled at the start of this chapter that Ashley had experienced the liturgy of the Eucharist. By such a symbolic feeding, Christians of many kinds recall the Last Supper of Jesus with his original followers. The meal has changed decidedly, with layers of religious ceremonial having been added. But when the original purpose is reconsidered, stark truth leaps out. One need not understand, or accept, theological explanations of the ceremony. But one can embrace the symbolic meal itself and grasp its implications for one's life.

The need to be fed and the possibility of being fed in community are dramatically portrayed. In the process, a sense of being bound together, uniquely and powerfully, can arise. Not every liturgy can speak to every person. But on each occasion there is a powerful, implied invitation: you can be a part, you can join in. You can be fed, and, if you wish, you can go further by taking part in this lively expression of faith community. By such steps belief is lived. You begin to speak of "growth," with trust as a key component. That is, while your questions continue, and perhaps intensify, belief seems possible because belief must be lived, and you have begun to live it. Belonging is the doorway to belief.

A long time ago a choir member in a New England church liked to chide his minister: "What if I don't recite the creed, and don't even like it? Can I remain in the choir?" Each time the minister would smile and say: "Of course you can." The minister knew, and so did the choir member, that belief begins with participation. Not a static quality, belief is dynamic. It is a journey, though hardly a clear and straight line. All the activities of a congregation, and not just worship, can be avenues toward belief.

Ideally belief can be shaped in any aspect of a congregation's life. In recent years, for example, there has been attention to infusing clear spiritual purpose into committees and boards that are common to congregations. Even the most ordinary discussion can prompt enhanced belief, if conducted with personal as well as organizational sensitivity. Certainly programs of study or of aid to the hungry and jobless can strengthen belief as a by-product. The reason is easily understood. When congregations function as they should, every facet of their common life points toward belief.

Trust is the basis of belief, and trust increases when congregational life proceeds in healthy ways reflective of the ideals of faith community. Belief is possible, and becomes enhanced, when trust deepens and there are clear links to tenets of faith tradition. We depict trust as the awakening of possibility. Trust is activity that embodies words, action that realizes ideals. Deep trust honors people, and even invites their better selves to emerge. People being frail, trust can be disappointed and falter. But trust can also be resilient, and so extend fresh invitations to hope together. Of course, trust is also an act of leadership, taking the risk that stated intentions will become reality. When that happens, belief takes life. "Truthiness" emerges, and you can give your heart to it, because you trust it.

We must not assume that this only happens within the church walls. Belief can happen anywhere. If we make it a requirement to darken the door of a church, then we've placed a serious limitation on the accessibility and exploration of belief. But this raises the difficult question, how do we do this?

At West End Collegiate Church, we recently started a Pub Theology night as an experiment to meet this challenge. It meets at one of the local pubs, and each month a small group gathers and discusses a different theological or biblical topic. In one sense there seems nothing earthshaking about getting together, discussing theology, and having a beer. But one quickly discovers that because you're not on your turf, you can't set the terms for discussion. The views expressed are wide-ranging and at times cherished beliefs are challenged. Those who want to force conversation to Christian conclusions will be greatly frustrated. But for those who are open to an unfettered exploration of belief with people who may not be interested in attending church, it is an enriching and eye-opening experience. For those interested in starting a group, we commend Byran Berghoef's *Pub Theology: Beer, Conversation, and God.*[41] It is helpful in understanding the basis and possibilities of this approach.

This experiment thus far has proved successful in providing a new place for our members to explore their faith, but it has also attracted newcomers who do not attend our church. What surprised us most are the demographics. We thought this initiative would attract the younger crowd, partly because it was started by our young, hip associate pastor. However, it attracts those from the age of twenty to seventy. It is too early to tell what the outcome will be, but it has proven to be a way to provide safe space in the public sphere to explore belonging and belief. The staff at the local pub think it is so cool that they provide a meeting place—and an occasional free drink!

Belonging and believing do not occur simply or readily. Even as they belong, there will be many people, including choir members, who must push back. They have to believe in idiosyncratic ways. But even as they wrestle with belief, they become part of it. The magic of being part of a community has captured their hearts.

CHAPTER FIVE

The Magic of Community

When Community Happens

The noise quickly becomes deafening. Tens of thousands of people are gathering to watch their hometown team play. As they do, there is a palpable sense of energy in the stadium. Filing into their seats, refreshments in hand, they have come to be thrilled. Each of them seems to be wearing something red, the team's home colors. Some are dressed entirely in red; a few have their faces painted. More than spectators, they are participants, even an extension of the team on the field, as they envision it. They have waited anxiously for this afternoon and now the game is finally near. At this moment nothing else matters. Nothing matters except their anticipation for the team to appear and the competition to begin.

Then suddenly the team streams onto the field. As they do, even amid the din of cheering, a familiar tune begins over the public address system. Momentarily there is a sudden hush sweeping over the throng. Then, as one, they join in singing lustily:

> When you walk through a storm,
> Hold your head up high,
> And don't be afraid of the dark
>
> At the end of the storm,
> Is a golden sky,
> And the sweet silver song of the lark
>
> Walk on through the wind,
> Walk on through the rain,
> Though your dreams be tossed and blown
>
> Walk on walk on with hope in your heart,
> And you'll never walk alone,
> You'll never walk alone.

The last line is repeatedly sung, until the crowd seems exhausted. "You'll never walk alone." Over and over, they sing. Finally, their allegiance to their team thoroughly expressed, they settle into seats, and await the game's beginning. But before long, especially if their team scores a goal, they burst forth again. "You'll never walk alone." Again and again, they sing it.

The words and tune are from a Rogers and Hammerstein musical, *Carousel*, which appeared on Broadway in 1945. How the song was perpetuated, and found its way to a distant stadium, is the stuff of legend. But the basis of its appeal is clear: this team and its fans form a community of enthusiasm for the sport and support for each other. There is a bond, a sense of common purpose that is captured by the words. The music and the lyrics become the rivets that bind this community together. Simply hearing the tune, or humming the words, creates an electric feeling, and the sense of being part of something worthwhile larger than oneself.

As they sing, many fans wave banners and twirl caps. Clad in scarves, shirts, and jackets of the team's colors, they jump and sway as they sing. Some wipe away tears, a few weep profusely. The sense of identification with this ream runs deep. The feeling of being united in support evokes profound emotion. The power of belonging in this moment is stunning.

The team is Liverpool, one of England's best professional football (soccer) clubs. The scene is Anfield Stadium, the team's home. Typically over 45,000 people pack the stadium, and thousands more watch or listen to the game by various media. Long ago Liverpool adopted "You'll Never Walk Alone" as their anthem, and something of a motto. It is emblazoned over one of the main gates to the stadium. But it is not only Liverpool; the fans in other stadiums can be heard bursting into the song as they cheer on their teams. There is a resonance between the song and their affinity for the team and its championship hopes. Something about the team and the song speak to a deep allegiance, and a need for belonging, among them. Somehow they link themselves to this team and to each other through the team. The song expresses deep hope.

A third habit of incarnational people is "the habit of *living among,* which means *participating in the natural activities of the culture around you with whimsical holiness.*"

Matt Smay and Hugh Halter

Paraphrased from *The Tangible Kingdom: Creating Incarnational Community*

Community often forms around sports teams. Some deep personal aspiration is tapped, a striving for accomplishment and recognition and even glory is invoked. One discovers that others hold the same longing for community, for the place where they can belong. There are ways to explain this allegiance, many quite simple: the team represents the place where you grew up, or the team's colors or style of play or a star player attract interest. In any case, the longing to be part of something dynamic and exciting, something one can share with others, is apparent.

Some teams speak of their widespread followings as "nations." Websites sell gear, in team colors, especially clothing. Virtually anything to make public announcement of one's loyalty is available. Websites also offer recent team news, notes on upcoming games and public events featuring team players. There is always reference to fan club activities. No team of any caliber, professional or amateur or scholastic, is complete without extensive marketing of itself. There are millions of people waiting to be drawn into the community that supports a team.

For many people the belonging they seek unites them in a vast wave of support for some form of athletics. Stadium noise is impressive proof, as is the variety of sports trinkets. But noise also is the product of other sorts of belonging; other communities of people also are defined by their special interest, and one expression of it is noise, even without a large stadium.

Outside a suburban café one Sunday morning, the noise is deafening as a different sort of community gathers. They are members of a sports car club, devotees of an expensive European make. No more than two dozen cars appear, but the roar of their arrival proves deafening. Some owners appear dramatically, complete with squealing tires loudly as they stop. Others let their engines' throaty rumble speak even after their cars are parked. At last, one by one, they are silent. Drivers and some passengers drift into the café for brunch.

Rather than disperse in the café, they seize a section of the dining room. The ritual is well practiced. One club member drapes a banner with the car's crest onto the mantel. Most members in attendance can be identified by their shirts and caps, announcing their preferred car. There is warm chatter once brunch is ordered: the club members have their own language, featuring talk of parts, models of cars, recent races, and styles of driving. Their brunch is leisurely, but their conversations are loud and energetic. Finally, reluctantly, in groups of twos and threes, they bid their good-byes, remind each other of the next meeting, and drift away. One by one, throbbing engines and squealing tires peel away.

For some people today, community is readily found. By various means they have discovered particular interests and people with whom to pursue them. It is to be expected that someone has multiple interests—in effect, multiple identities—defined by several communities. The rabid sports fan one day is an avid sports car driver the next. Affinity groups abound, offering the feeling of belonging in particular ways.

Inevitably a path to defining one's self at a deep level appears. One's interests may reveal deep hopes and concerns, otherwise hidden personal talents, and cherished opportunities for self-expression. Development of the interest likely takes time and money and cultivation of ability. Car lovers tinker with their vehicles to sharpen performance, or simply to maintain them. Soon lovers of the same car, or the same team, are found; community is built and relationships form. They are circumscribed in some ways, meeting only periodically and focused largely on the particular interest. But the sense of belonging is profound. Community has been born.

A New Intentionality

Community has become a precious experience. It involves the magic of discovering that others share your interests. Others embrace similar hopes and speak the language you speak.

Other people define portions of their lives by a pursuit that engages you. Community entails shared beliefs, experiences, needs, intentions, abilities, and hopes. Community structures one's time and resources, not merely to build the interest one has developed, but to do so in tandem with other people. There one finds support and reinforcement of one's values and lifestyle. Community becomes a precious commodity.

But community today is increasingly different from what it once was. Once community was inherited; it was the place where you were born, and the way of life that was handed to you. There was little sense of choice; what is most at stake in any sense of community, namely your identity, was given. You could rebel, and for a time many people did, leaving home for education or military service or work. It may not have seemed like rebellion, but it was the way you struck out on your own, to prove yourself and to discover yourself.

Eventually, however, you came home, for there was a clear sense of what was "home." It was where you belonged. It was where you fit in, where people were like you. Once, or so we imagine, you could walk into a job, likely one with which your family was already associated. The company or the firm promised you a career, without the thought of ever changing firms or companies. In some cases, you had to move, if it was a larger company. But you longed to come back, and eventually you did. You saw the world; then it was time to come home where you belonged. Community was a given.

Over the past generation, that sense of coming home has eroded in two respects. For some people there never was a sense of home; their family was disrupted or there was little family to begin with. Ben speaks of growing up in a military family, where there was constant movement. Then his parents divorced. What's home for Ben? He chuckles and says, "Colorado, because that's where we were the longest. But I graduated from high school in Michigan, so I don't know."

On the other hand, the community into which one was born may have changed sharply. Ann speaks longingly of the California suburb in which she grew up. "It was all Irish Catholic then; now I think it's all Armenian or something like that. I have no reason to go back."

While one of us was attending a conference, we were asked to draw a picture that represented our lives. One woman, because of the amount of moving she had done in her life, drew a picture of a plant with no roots. She said with tears in her eyes, "I drew this because I have no roots. I have no place to call home." She is representative of a growing number of people, whether the uprootedness is physical or metaphorical. With the increasing number of fractured and highly mobile lives, we must not miss the implications for ministry.

Forty-one percent of Americans do not live in the state in which they were born.

Unites States Census Bureau

The result is that community cannot be presumed; it must be found. Community must arise around something that marks us as individuals, yet gives a basis for being with one another. Further, community is less understood as a place, and less seen as part of life's daily flow. The community experience of old entailed work and school and civic groups, and certainly being the member of a religious congregation. Now community is less defined as a *vocation*, or one's daily work and responsibilities. Rather, community arises as an *avocation*, that is, individual interests that are likely removed from what one does to earn a living and where one lives physically.

This is not to say that work cannot entail community. Many companies now emphasize team building or ways to encourage both effective performance and job satisfaction in the company of others. At one large electronic chain store, for example, one commonly finds sales consultants working together to help customers find the right electronic device and to launch its operation. Other teams stand ready to offer classes on one's device and to repair it when it falters. At its best, the workplace also can offer the magic of community.

But community is defined as more of an avocation today. Many people are thoroughly immersed in work, but most people long for time to pursue personal interests with those who share them. In that sense, community now is an ideal that is chosen personally. It arises amid activities one pursues outside the routine of daily necessity. There is a longing to be part of something larger than oneself, in the company of people who understand. The varieties of such experiences and the sense of community they prompt seem infinite. From the outside, many people seem to belong in multiple ways. But as fulfilling as it can prove, it still seems incomplete. Sports teams and car clubs, and countless other avocations, consume many people, apparently happily. Yet something is missing, and many other people lack any such attachment. For many people today, community appears in fleeting form, if it appears at all.

One instance of fleeting community can be found at an urban bar where every Thursday night is "jazz night." A live combo appears, usually the same musicians, though some float in and out, and the music begins by 9 p.m. Jazz lovers are drawn there and over time have built friendships. Bart goes every Thursday, turning down invitations that conflict. Sure enough, as we enter, the music blaring, people approach him. There are warm hugs, a few quips and jokes, then bar stools and drink orders. The music is deafening and introductions must be shouted.

"You'll like Wayne," Bart bellows over a saxophone. "For Wayne this is church." So it seemed. On the next stool, Wayne was raptly listening, pausing only to greet a few people and to get another drink. When the band took a break, Bart and Wayne worked the room, revealing details about people in the crowd. "Charlene is a nurse, I think. Denny works for a package delivery service. Hank got laid off but has some interviews. Judy is going through a divorce." Several wave upon hearing their names mentioned. There was genuine care in the details that were conveyed. If there was community here, it was because of Bart and Wayne.

But to what extent was it community? Certainly the bar was a gathering spot, a place "where everybody knows your name," as an old television program depicted. The connection between people was genuine and beneficial. They know each other's names and something of each other's story. But "community" remained at a certain level, and that was an aspect of its appeal. People could come and go as they chose. They could reveal as much or as little about themselves as they wished. If they desired, they need never return. For a time they would be missed, but their spot at the bar would be filled. If they returned, there would be a friendly welcome. It would be their choice.

All of these forms of community are familiar to Ashley. She had tried most of them. She did not know Bart or Wayne, or the Thursday night jazz club gathering. But she had her own version. She had been to college and professional sports, without knowing a thing about the Liverpool squad. She was not interested in European sports cars, but other sorts of interests had drawn more than passing interest at times. She had tried them all and found all offered some gratification. She was in no way negative. But she was looking for more.

When Community Means Change

There are various forms of belonging today, all of which point to one or another kind of community. By implicit understanding among those who participate, any community offers certain benefits and brings certain limitations. Whether it's a favorite sports team, or a special interest or hobby group, or a local watering hole, people find a common bond. They discover mutuality of a sort, and it can prove meaningful. Ask the people in attendance, and they will tell you their lives are better because they are there.

But there will be limits and usually those are understood and accepted. For each person who participates in one activity, there will likely be other interests and related groups and events. Some of these groups today will be virtual, given the dramatic growth of social media. Other groups, actual or virtual, will be episodic, even at one's own whim, given the fluidity of community today. Blending various forms of occasional community creates life as the sort of personalized quilt many people today want. "I don't put all my eggs in one basket," Bart comments at the bar. Many people wish for nothing more.

Even for people who now envision community in multiple forms, there likely was a phase of life when community was more encompassing and more definitive of their identities. The experience of community is integral to times of intense change, and everyone will face such moments. One example is education, especially times of higher education and especially entry into a profession. The intense training affords community for those taking this path together.

With a sense of shared struggle, students in professional schools orient their lives around the assimilation of knowledge and the honing of practical skills. In the process their personalities and social interactions are stamped decisively. Similarly recruits entering military service face a grueling period as they are pushed to new physical and mental limits. In the midst of the regimen, bonds of community arise. They are going through something worthwhile with one another.

Together their former lives are stripped away and a new, common life is shaped. The recruits who endure the ordeal discover a sense of belonging they will recall proudly for the rest of their lives. They may have experienced various forms of community previously; now they have been changed and built a bond that is permanent. They feel they have discovered the deep meaning of belonging, together, through intense struggle.

> I define *connection as the energy that exists between people when they feel seen, heard, and valued; when they can give and receive without judgment; and when they derive sustenance and strength from the relationship.*
>
> **Brené Brown**
>
> *The Gifts of Imperfection: Let Go of Who You Think You're Supposed to Be and Embrace Who You Are*

These illustrations offer a crucial clue to how belonging gains substance and becomes more than episodic. Belonging moves to a deeper level in a community where personal and shared change occurs. The emphasis on emerging as enhanced people together sharpens the meaning of belonging. It is more than being present occasionally, or partially, however warm the experience. When belonging arises among people committed to decisive change, lasting personal and shared possibility surfaces. A new way of life is at hand, a new way of seeing and engaging the world is within reach.

Given such profound implications, community of this sort, and the belonging it fosters, exerts unusual power. Yet in spite of the benefit this can produce, enhancing individual lives and fostering lasting bonds of community, some people hesitate. It is not simply a matter of finding that one is not suited to a particular program or career or vocational path. For some such intense focus is too high a psychological price to pay, even if they are capable of paying it. Increasing numbers of people resist any effort by external authority to define who they are. The surrender of individuality is too much of a demand, even to fulfill the promise of individual reward.

The fear is especially apparent among adolescents and young adults. The transition from education to adulthood is proving extended and rocky for many. Economic downturns increase the uncertainty and the feeling of personal vulnerability. Many young adults long to give their lives to large issues and causes; they imagine addressing significant challenges with others who share such passion.

But there is reluctance to entrust one's self to others, even for what one already holds dear. The feeling of risk is too great; commitment proves too difficult to sustain. Whether in education or work, and certainly in relationships and group affiliations, belonging seems too steep a hill to climb. Community must be loose, floating, even tentative. The ability to duck in or out as one chooses becomes the main criterion for one's participation. Even then, after a time, some people move on, for the sake of moving on. Committing oneself wholeheartedly long term proves difficult. A surrender of one's individuality seems involved, and the imagined loss of self is too big a demand. The promise of belonging goes unfulfilled.

The Fear of Not Belonging

At the same time, paradoxically, there are numerous people who are ready to be defined by external authority. If the price of belonging is too high for some, the fear of not belonging is too severe a challenge for others. If some people fear the loss of individuality, other people surrender themselves readily to authoritarian forms of community. The appeal of being shaped so conclusively with others can be the source of both remarkable benefit and striking harm.

Over the past generation there have been frightening instances of belonging, and images of religious community gone awry. On November 18, 1978, a charismatic leader named Jim Jones led 912 people in a mass suicide at their cult's settlement in a jungle in Guyana. A member of Congress who had come to investigate the cult was killed along with members of his team. Jones's group had begun as an independent religious congregation in Indianapolis, then migrated to California, then to South America.

On a smaller scale, though just as violent, a fundamentalist religious compound in Waco, Texas, burned after a prolonged stalemate then gunfight with federal officials. The date was April 19, 1993, and 76 people, including children, died. Among the dead was David Koresh, founder and charismatic leader of the group he named the Branch Davidians. They had built a rambling structure outside Waco and armed themselves in anticipation of an apocalyptic assault. Sadly they designed their fate.

Still smaller in scale, and less public in its violence, but no less tragic, 36 members of a cult gathered in a San Diego suburb died together on March 26, 1997. They called themselves Heaven's Gate, and they took their own lives together amid the community they had created. Their leader, Marshall Applewhite, had persuaded his followers that by taking their lives they would migrate to an alien spacecraft that had approached earth in the wake of a comet passing by this planet. As astonishing as this idea seemed, Applewhite readily joined his followers in carrying it out. The power of their belonging overwhelmed the illogic of their ideas.

Fortunately the number of such horrific experiences of belonging is tiny. But short of such conflagrations, the number of controversial and authoritarian groups can be multiplied.

Inevitably there are religious overtones if not explicitly religious claims. Even when violent conclusions do not occur, accusations of harm to participants can surface. In 2008, for example, Warren Jeffs, leader of the Fundamentalist Church of Jesus Christ of Latter-Day Saints, was convicted in a Texas court and sentenced to a term of life plus twenty years. The conviction followed several years of legal proceedings, and intense media coverage, in which Jeffs was accused of having raped teenage girls. It was clear that he had become the charismatic leader of a cultlike Mormon offshoot, a movement largely of his own design. From the following he built, Jeffs selected multiple "wives," by whom he fathered children. Yet some of the "wives" were teenage girls who were psychologically manipulated and sexually coerced.

Controversy and accusations have followed other novel religious groups. For example, calling itself a church, Scientology is an organization that teaches and applies concepts devised by the late L. Ron Hubbard. A writer and dabbler in psychology, Hubbard concluded that people could be freed from the influence of painful experiences. Guided by practitioners in personal and group sessions, individuals are led toward Scientology's view of healthy living, cleared of the stain of trauma. They are also drawn into a group identity that can become all-embracing. More than a way toward becoming "clear," Scientology is a community of those who have been freed.

More than its techniques, Scientology has acquired a public image of steadily enclosing individuals into lives withdrawn from the wider world. Amid controversies this has encouraged, Scientology's claims to be a religion and to overcome personal pain have been questioned, notably by journalist Lawrence Wright in his book *Going Clear*.[42] Links between Scientology and the entertainment industry, as well as its seemingly vast resources have also prompted scrutiny.

At the very least, Scientology attests to the extent of the need to belong, and the depth of the need for healing in the company of others that many people pursue. The drive to break free of the past and to find lasting change can become all-consuming. But when in a person's life does this drive go too far? The tenor of this question surrounds Scientology and other novel religious movements. Can we distinguish between desired forms of belonging and forms that may produce more harm than good?

Healthy vs. Unhealthy Belonging

In *Strong Religion*, Scott Appleby and his colleagues Gabriel Almond and Emmanuel Sivan probe the characteristics of fundamentalist and sectarian religious movements today.[43] They find, as we have discovered, an emphasis on change that becomes a group's basis. But change is expressed through rejection, and sometimes hostility, toward the wider world. Developing a set of teachings, usually from an authoritarian founder, the group creates psychological and even physical barriers to keep the rest of the world out, and to keep group members in. To some extent group participants accept this approach, if only in theory.

The intention is rarely simply to dominate or to subdue people. The group arises, and gains a following, because it fosters a vision. The founder's teachings present what one author calls an "imagined community." A select few people can know the truth and live genuinely apart from the world's distractions. Becoming an "enclave community," as Appleby and his colleagues describe, the group turns inward, focusing on creating social order as it presumes true order must be. But such intensity arises that conflict and controversy within or without the group are likely. The "imagined community" with its promise of change can become restrictive and harmful.[44]

It is important to note that every religious or quasi-religious group or organization can prompt forms of belonging that turn destructive. This is no more startling than saying that clubs or groups or companies and businesses can harbor unhealthy dynamics. It is no more than saying that families, or human relations of all sorts, can breed suspicion and discord. The dismaying feature of religious groups is that claims of beneficial change and images of healthy community can be betrayed in practice. Some religions seem prone, even poised, for such contradiction. Others, especially historic expressions of religious tradition, must be alert to realities in their midst that threaten the integrity of their ideals.

The reason such issues arise today is simple: there is a restless, widespread search for belonging. Inherited forms of belonging either have eroded or no longer suffice; most people are not content with accepting the life circumstances that were given to them. Many people seek a way to belong that is their choice, a way that expresses something authentic of themselves. Many want to feel that they can change and want to do so in a community of people who understand.

In the wider world there is uncertainty and confusion. Perhaps the right choices, and the right community of people, somehow can change the world's ills to a better future. But how would one recognize the right sort of community? What are the markers of healthy relations, of the best sort of belonging? What would set it apart?

Ashley had wondered this often. There seemed to be many groups and many interests, many promises of healing, many groups and teachers. She enjoyed times of fun and events with friends. But she needed something more. She was wary of groups that seemed too intense, that seemed to cut people off from others. She was also puzzled by so many religious claims and groups, most of which made no sense to her. How could she know the right sort of community? How could she belong in the right sort of way?

For Ashley, there is latent yearning for another kind of "imagined community," but it is not marked by isolation, restrictive views, or fear. Instead it is marked by its inclusiveness and eagerness to engage those who are different. Her latent desire to be a part of something larger creates a yearning to be a part of a community that is marked by diversity rather than its sameness.

> Dominator culture has tried to keep us all afraid, to make us choose safety instead of risk, sameness instead of diversity. Moving through that fear, finding out what connects us, revelling in our differences; this is the process that brings us closer, that gives us a world of shared values, of meaningful community.
>
> **Bell Hooks**
>
> *Teaching Community: A Pedagogy of Hope*

One of the challenges this desire for diversity presents to congregations is that education programs typically have been to engender the same views on faith and life rather than invite diverse expressions. Increasingly congregations will have to find ways to encourage and expose people to a broad range of views rather than an "authorized" version of which the church views itself as the keeper.

One way congregations are beginning to address the desire for diversity is by including interfaith engagement as part of faith formation. One such approach is Scriptural Reasoning (SR). SR is the practice of a small group of people from different faiths, usually Judaism, Christianity, and Islam, who gather to read their scriptures together. It is something both of us have hosted and participated in through our congregations and seminaries. (More about the specifics of the program can be found at scripturalreasoning.org.) Through the process of reading and seeking to understand one another's texts, one's understanding of one's own faith is deepened while growing in understanding of another's faith. And through it all, the relationships between people are deepened. Unlike many other interfaith programs, it allows people to speak from the heart of their traditions rather than avoid their distinctiveness, lest they offend someone.

Initiatives like SR will need to be incorporated into our approach to faith development in the future as we move out of a reformational paradigm into a paradigm of religious pluralism. Once the reigning question was, "Who is the true Church?" with little attention given to other religions. Now people live in religiously plural communities and have little interest in which brand of Christianity is right. They want to know how their faith relates to that of their neighbors. It will soon be imperative for us to help people make sense of their faith in relation to other faith traditions. It becomes a marker of healthy community in that it helps people relate positively to the diversity of people around them and not seclude themselves from them. We have more to say about this in the next chapter.

Guided by Compassion

[Jesus] said also to the one who had invited him, "When you give a luncheon or a dinner, do not invite your friends or your brothers or your relatives or rich neighbors, in case they may invite you in return, and you would be repaid. But when you give a banquet, invite the poor, the crippled, the lame, and the blind. And you will be blessed, because they cannot repay you, for you will be repaid at the resurrection of the righteous." (Luke 14:12–14)

A different sort of community gathers every Sunday evening in a church basement. At first blush there seems to be little in common among the more than one hundred people who filter in. Some sit quietly, even reflectively. Others pace and await the arrival of someone they know. Many seem well practiced in the routine of the occasion, others seek direction. Warm greetings emerge as people gather, much like a bar or club. Soon there are various conversations, some from small clusters, some among the group preparing the large room. A variety of styles of dress and ages are present; a handful of children also romp around the room.

Community would seem to rely on people being alike. If they embrace the same sports team or sports car, they tend to dress alike. If they join a tightly defined religious or spiritual group, they are encouraged, even compelled, to hold the same beliefs. Most notions of belonging center on being alike. In that sense, it is easy to mistake belonging and fitting in. But belonging in the true sense is different, and so is the sort of community where true belonging is found. Life defined by Christian faith is journey toward belonging in a different sort of community.

What does this mean in practice? What does it mean for people to step forward, in the midst of their personal journeys, to build community of a different sort? How do the ideals and beliefs of Christianity encourage another way of people being together? How does this new community look?

In this chapter we have described community in two broad ways: first, occasional gatherings based on common interest; second, focused emphasis on personal change grounded in group exclusivity and regimentation. Both types have great appeal today, and both can offer personal and shared benefits, though profound shortcomings can surface in both.

From a distance the Sunday evening church gathering could resemble the other types of belonging. It does appear that people can flow in and out as they choose. Because it is a church, however, some could fear that the event could entice participants into accepting certain religious dogmas and authority figures. Both perceptions have grains of truth: people are free to attend or not attend, and the event grows out of the church's faith. But a closer look reveals a different community with a different approach to belonging. At this weekly event, the purpose is to build care for one another among people who seem profoundly different from one another.

This idea is not boldly expressed. No teaching or sermon is offered. No references to what one should believe or what ideas and groups one should reject will be heard. The emphasis is not on being alike, or on being set apart in an exclusive group. Instead the emphasis simply is on being together. So, with no fanfare, each Sunday one congregation offers an evening meal. Large cans welcome donations, but there is no required charge. A few volunteers are present to guide newcomers while other volunteers prepare the meal. Otherwise there is no structure. By 6:30 p.m. a buffet line has formed and is moving ahead. People filter among twenty-five tables, each with six chairs. By 7 p.m. most of the spots are taken.

Some sitting down to eat have attended a prayer service in the church; others have appeared only for dinner. The appeal is obvious: a meal is offered for which one need not pay or do anything. But something deeper is occurring: people are discovering one another in a way that otherwise would be unlikely. They are drawn together not because of interests or allegiances; they are drawn together in the midst of their obvious differences, to find and share their common humanity. Even so, it would not seem to be a particularly religious gathering. But overhearing the conversations that arise, one senses a new sort of community being shaped. People are testing a kind of belonging they may not have found before this simple meal.

"I'm Ruth," a woman at one table says unexpectedly. She had been eating quietly before her sudden introduction. "I'm new here; I came from San Diego." At first no one seems to know how to respond. Napkins, cups, and forks are shuffled nervously. Then another person ventures forth: "I'm Frank. I used to live in New Jersey; then I came here to live with my son and his family." Several others echo bits of their own stories. Martha is a divorced mother of two young daughters; Bob and Cynthia live nearby and heard this was a good occasion, even though church was not something they had thought about for years.

Then Sarah ventured a thought. "We all had something bring us here. Listening to all of you makes me think, life is not easy." "Not at all," Ruth adds emphatically. "Oh yeah," Martha says, embracing a crying child. "Well, you're lucky to have family," Carmen declares. She had listened intently, at times reacting silently with dramatic facial expressions. "Somewhere I have a son, but I haven't seen him in years." There is silence as this sad admission is absorbed. In a clumsy way, one man tries to help: "Invite him here and we'll talk to him."

Gradually, tentatively, the word "we" surfaces. Being at the same table, revealing bits of personal stories, the outline of a bond among the group appears. It is more than shared beliefs or experiences; it is a common hunger for meaning. It entails learning to speak openly, to seek direction, to gain acceptance. The meal is a vehicle to acknowledging and addressing common human needs, for overcoming human hurt. By small steps isolation recedes, community appears.

Something similar has already happened among the people who prepare and serve the meal. They represent a community that has developed further; they have made a commitment to be there, at least periodically, and to work together. Taking this step means that they have sensed the possibility the Sunday evening gatherings embody. But in no sense do they all think alike. Each has brought different personal needs and a different personal vision of how the meal should be organized. Several tend to express their views strongly.

"If it's not vegetarian, I don't want to cook. I'm outta here," Sally declares in the kitchen as the preparation team assembles. David adds, "I grew up Jewish and I won't touch pork." Fortunately the meals program has a committee, and each week there is a chair who represents the committee. This week it is Pam. "Nope, no pork," she says. "And if you like, you two can help Joe with the black bean burgers, or see if Luke needs help with the salad." There is silent assent and work proceeds.

Quickly large bowls of food take shape, and dispensers of water and lemonade are set out. A formidable coffee pot rumbles to life nearby. "Don't forget the decaf," someone yells to no one in particular. "And hot water for tea," another voice injects. Clearly there are a range of needs to be met. But meeting needs is the basis of the meal, and the community it builds.

In *Heaven's Kitchen*, Courtney Bender describes how community arises in such settings.[45] For her doctoral research she joined a team regularly serving meals in a feeding program in New York City. Her presenting question was: How do people practice religion in their everyday lives? Joining the "God's Love We Deliver" program for a year, serving especially persons with AIDS, Bender made a striking discovery: attention to the most basic human needs opens up complex layers of possibility. Personal meanings, personal hopes and fears, blend into shared experience. As practical tasks surface on the way to serving meals, forms of organization are negotiated. By sustaining and sharpening the process, the group makes the transition to community, as she expresses it. There is a sense of belonging rooted in service of others. In a word, the group focuses on *compassion*. They do not analyze compassion, or debate its theological or social or historical roots. They do not arrive at doctrinal standards for it, and may rarely even use the word. But it is what they are living. They are practicing tangible compassion, and seek ways to understand it and their role in it after the fact.

Friction continues to surface. They will never be like-minded in every respect. Nor will their temperaments always blend seamlessly. Visions of what it means and how it should be done still clash. And some on the team will arrive in the midst of personal challenges and simply feeling glum. Debates will surface occasionally about the reasons for the work. Some will say their religious convictions or spiritual quests have deepened. Others will simply report that they have done a good thing. There is no prescribed personal outcome.

Along the way, most doing the work and most in attendance report that they leave the meals better than they arrived. People who become regulars speak of teamwork and purpose in warm tones. They reveal a common language that has arisen among them, citing tasks they have performed and inserting stories about the people with whom they performed them. They may not see it, but they have begun to write a common story, focused on care. It is new, even daunting for some. It is still tentative, and not all of them fully trust it, or each other. But each time they go, community gains strength among them. Something has been awakened in them and something is being built. It surprises most of them as much as it excites and frightens them. In a way that is new and different for most, they find that life-giving community is possible. They can belong.

As alluring as it is, such community remains a struggle. Some people will only participate while keeping their eyes open for ways to leave. There is a widespread fear of commitment; there is also a restlessness to be ready for the next possibility. Social scientists have identified fear of any sort of commitment in some people, leading to regular changes in work, relationships, and places of residence. Explanations of such restlessness focus on fear of lost options, or fear of being unduly hindered or defined. For such people, who may be legion, everyday decisions can become burdens. Feelings of uncertainty and doubt readily surface. Passivity and doubt become the basis of a lifestyle.

Thus for many people, there are obstacles toward forming community. Even the preparation of a meal can demand patience and negotiation. It becomes clear that community at its best must blend people who are different, and who express themselves vigorously. Difference is the greatest challenge of all on the path to community.

CHAPTER SIX

Belonging without Walls

The Lord appeared to Abraham by the oaks of Mamre, as he sat at the entrance of his tent in the heat of the day. He looked up and saw three men standing near him. When he saw them, he ran from the tent entrance to meet them, and bowed down to the ground. He said, "My lord, if I find favor with you, do not pass by your servant. Let a little water be brought, and wash your feet, and rest yourselves under the tree. Let me bring a little bread, that you may refresh yourselves, and after that you may pass on—since you have come to your servant." So they said, "Do as you have said." (Genesis 18:1–5)

Do not neglect to show hospitality to strangers, for by doing that some have entertained angels without knowing it. (Hebrews 13:2)

Unprecedented Difference

The path toward belonging today is fraught with difficulty. As we have seen, people of all ages, but especially young adults like Ashley, approach belonging gingerly. Unsure of where or how they fit generally, they are especially wary of religion and congregations. They are fearful of being coerced spiritually and psychologically. There are significant examples of religious leaders and organizations acting abusively. This reality tells many young adults that religion in all forms is to be avoided. The idea of belonging does not occur readily.

But barriers to belonging can begin to crumble, as we have shown. Perhaps there is a small group or simply a few friends wanting to build understanding together. They find that exploring belonging becomes a journey along which belief becomes possible. As rich as the personal discoveries can be, the surprise of finding wholeness with other people can be a shock. It is possible to build community, and to see for oneself what belonging offers. In fact, the reality of belonging is grounded in the discovery that "I" am incomplete without "you." Almost without saying it, "we" arises. Tentatively a new, shared identity hatches.

It is an awkward identity at first. Its worth must be unfolded and tested and sustained. For congregations, the intention would seem apparent; seemingly they want to proclaim and to live their beliefs in ways that draw people in search of belonging. But congregations like all human groups reveal their character not in what they say but in what they do. Confessional statements or affiliation with larger religious organizations mean little to the Ashleys of our time. Rather, the practices, that is, the patterns and activities of religious life in local contexts are what matter.

Congregations readily focus their energies on meetings and memoranda and resolutions. They pay inordinate attention to processes that can lead nowhere, while ignoring the basic reasons they exist. When they do, Ashley and her peers leave quickly, if they ever bothered to enter. They have little interest in resolutions or meetings or statements; they wonder how the world becomes better because of institutional narcissism. This is not how they want to belong.

> We used to be a group of revolutionaries. Now we're a group of *resolutionaries.*
>
> **The Reverend Lillian Daniel**
>
> Spoken after a General Synod meeting

However, she takes notice when congregations feed hungry people and house those who are homeless. Work projects such as refurbishing houses for poor people or supporting medical and social initiatives pique her interest. Discussion groups that encourage honest, even cynical questions also appeal. She also notices that congregation members volunteer to make such programs possible. She then sees that profound forms of belonging emerge from working and discussing together.

Bonds are built as genuine, even urgent human needs are addressed. The need to belong is fed when one feeds others. A spiritual symmetry between doing, belonging, and believing takes shape and Ashley senses its appeal. It is possible to belong and to believe in ways that are dynamic and have wide benefit. Her life is enhanced as she enhances others. A sense of purpose sharpens, and she finds there are ideals she can affirm because she has seen them in practice. These ideals are not a set of doctrines or institutional rules, she muses; this path simply is true.

Still there is another major obstacle on the way to belonging. As human communities, and not simply religious organizations, congregations must face the reality of differ-ence. Communities of all sorts only arise when difference is encountered effectively. Congregations bear special responsi-bility because of the religious ideals they proclaim. To embody their faith, congregations must see difference as opportunity, not obstacle.

But this is a stiff challenge. Even among people who live in proximity, and bring inherent understanding for each oth-er's circumstances, difference also is apparent. Towns and urban neighborhoods and even rural areas are more diverse than even a generation ago, especially ethnically and racially. Even people of similar cultural backgrounds can represent a variety of needs and outlooks, as the team managing a Sunday evening meal discovered. Multiple needs, varied per-sonal stories, a spectrum of family situations, and simply dif-ferent approaches to even participating in an occasional meal all surfaced on the same occasion.

Even more, the spiritual and religious perceptions and questions among the group offered broad and often incom-patible priorities and views. Increasingly people approach con-gregations on the basis of restless personal journeys. Arrival in a congregation rarely signals they have reached a firm reli-gious or spiritual destination. Their journeys continue. The arrival can be momentary. Most hope that their experience in a congregation will fuel the search, not end it.

A New Religious Reality

Meanwhile, not surprisingly, many people explore multiple religious and spiritual sources at the same time. Ashley's good friend, Jan, would often race from helping with the Sunday meal to participating in a meditation group at a nearby Buddhist temple. Recently Jan participated in a wed-ding there and excitedly brought pictures to show Ashley. It was intriguing; Ashley resolved to learn more about Buddhism and others religions as well. There was no hint that she would cease exploring congregations. The two explorations would augment each other, and benefit her.

The urge to be fed by multiple spiritual sources at the same time is commonplace. Even a brief glance at the "religion" and "spirituality" sections of a bookstore, or book sales on a website, reveal a vast array of themes and sources. A further glance reveals that book sales are brisk. Add conferences, retreats, and workshops, displayed on hundreds of web and social media sites and fueled by themes from diverse faith traditions, and the urgency of the quest becomes plain.

This desire is captured in Paul Knitter's work *Without Buddha I Could Not Be a Christian.*[46] It has proven to resonate with many people because it reveals how his experience with another religion deepened and strengthen his Christian faith. As leaders we need to be aware of this exploration, exposing ourselves to other religious traditions and seeing how interaction with them can enhance our faith—rather then viewing them as the competition. We have on a number of occasions referred people to Knitter's work because parishioners have expressed their exposure to Buddhism, wondering how it might relate to their Christian faith. To be unequipped to respond risks having them drift away from the very place they wish to call home.

In chapter one, we noted that Ashley is not alone; an avid spiritual quest is happening today. It is not a new quest. Nearly a generation ago sociologist Wade Clark Roof described America as a "spiritual marketplace." Since he coined this memorable description, the reality of the spiritual search has not only deepened, it has broadened. Now the quest is focused on belonging with particular intensity; at the same time, it is a quest that presumes multiple sources. Searching, and even belonging, must be shaped by diverse religious and spiritual sources.

In part this shift in the nature and direction of the spiritual quest has arisen because Ashley and her peers approach religion and spirituality with the outlook of customers starting down a cafeteria line. Today they might choose mostly Asian foods. Tomorrow it could be Mexican or perhaps a salad of their own construction. The next day it could be grilled meat or fish, or a vegetarian Indian dish.

Similarly the faith journey has become something of a consumer experience. Every day offers a fresh exploration of variety, as one constructs it. Often the day's choices are impulsive. Consistently no one cuisine alone can suffice, and each day the blend differs. Somehow, in the search for ways to belong, there must be allowance for impulse and exploration. Belonging and believing as well must reflect appreciation of difference, the more varied the better.

In another sense this assumption that difference must be embraced, in the midst of finding a people and a place to belong, reflects more than a consumer mindset or rampant, aimless individualism. American life has reached an unprecedented level of cultural and religious difference. The most obvious illustration is the decline in the percentage of the population that defines itself as Christian. While a majority of over 70 percent says it is Christian, the figure was over 90 percent fifty years ago. Meanwhile membership in religious institutions of all sorts rests at about 50 percent, down from a peak of 70 percent a generation ago.[47]

In part as we have discussed, such figures represent the rise of the "Nones" in American life. The "Nones" are persons who claim no religious affiliation, but who are likely to hold baseline religious or spiritual interest. Less than one-third of them are atheists or agnostics, and their ranks show scant growth.[48]

As Ashley and her peers know well, the other reality behind the drop in the Christian majority is the rise of religious pluralism. Buddhism has become a particular source of fascination in American life. Estimates of the numbers of Buddhists, for example, defy accuracy, and claims for as many as five million Buddhists have been made. Recently one source has placed the American Buddhist population at over one million, based on participation in temples and immigrant populations from largely Buddhist countries.

> The United States is the most religiously diverse nation in the world.
>
> Diana Eck
>
> *A New Religious America*

At the same time Buddhism has become a cultural phenomenon of sorts, with untold numbers of people dabbling sufficiently to construct their own private versions. Buddhism's porous nature permits coming and going of a sort, typically with little regard for the content of belief or practice. Nor is there much regard for participation or belonging in substantial ways. Pop culture versions of Buddhism reflect individual whim and offer something of a contrast with the actual patterns of practice in largely Buddhist contexts. In various respects, then, Buddhism is growing in America.

If sheer growth is considered, Islam is expanding at a dramatic rate. Though estimates vary widely, perhaps five million or more Muslims now live in the United States. While Muslims are a slight percentage of the overall population, the expansion of Islam signifies what has likely been a doubling or more of Muslim adherents over the past generation. In large measure such growth reflects immigration, especially from South and Southeast Asia. But conversions to Islam are apparent, especially among young adults in the vicinity of college and university campuses. More than is the case with Buddhism, Islam invites a pattern of belonging, and the appeal of a clearly defined way of life in a community of faith.

The United States has long been seen as a beacon of religious freedom. From colonial times there has been a prized American emphasis on freedom to believe and to practice religion as one defines it, or to refuse to do so. In theory all faith communities are welcome and given opportunity to publish their convictions and honor their traditions to the fullest extent. In fact, this ideal has coexisted with de facto Christian dominance of the culture. Now the ideal of religious freedom is being tested as never before. Diana Eck, and other scholars of religious pluralism, have described how extensive the American religious spectrum has become. What is especially unprecedented is the spread of religious difference across the country.

In Virginia where one of us lives, for example, the Muslim population once was slight. Now it numbers over 500,000 and not only in the Washington, DC, suburbs. The greater Richmond area, with over 1.3 million persons, now includes upwards of ten mosques and perhaps 20,000 Muslims, a dramatic increase over the past generation.

The same pattern is being repeated in every metropolitan area of comparable size, and it is more than a Muslim reality. In cities such as Charlotte and Columbus, Kansas City and Atlanta, Denver and Indianapolis, the growth of religious and cultural difference is striking. The city streets and shopping malls reveal women in headscarves and men in turbans. There is the occasional monk in yellow robes and, more often, the bearded rabbi. Signs and other public announcements are in Spanish as well as English. And in a ride home from the airport one afternoon, a cab driver recently arrived from Ethiopia excitedly invites passengers to the new restaurant his cousin has opened. Long noticeable in New York, Chicago, and Los Angeles, this social reality now exists across the country. Ashley and her counterparts would be surprised not to live among such difference.

Consequently they are startled when they learn how extensive religious prejudice has become. A recent survey by the Gallup organization revealed that upwards of half of all Americans are suspicious, if not doggedly opposed, to Islam. They associate Muslims with extremism and threats of terrorist acts. Sadly, such prejudice is also apparent toward Jews, despite the American legacy of support for Israel. In some instances vandalism of places of worship and physical attacks against persons seen as different have occurred. In a few well publicized cases, there have been threats to burn the sacred texts of faith traditions, especially the Qur'an of Islam, and insulting videos have been uploaded to popular websites.

> For most of its existence, Christianity has been the most intolerant of worldfaiths, doing its best to eliminate all competitors, with Judaism a qualified exception, for which (thanks to some thoughts from Augustine of Hippo) it found space to serve its own theological and social purposes.
>
> **Diarmaid MacCulloch**
>
> *Christianity: The First Three Thousand Years*

The numbers of such instances, mercifully, have been few. But they cast an ugly shadow across the American ideal of religious freedom. Yet such incidents, however few, give Ashley and persons on her sort of quest reason to hesitate. As much as they seek a way to belong, they resist any suggestion, even the tiniest hint, that by belonging they disparage people who belong and believe in ways that are different from the way they have found. They intend to be fed by difference, not to avoid or condemn it.

Diversity 2.0

Religious leaders and organizations have been alert to the theme of difference for many years. Since the last quarter of the twentieth century, few ideals have been more prominent than "diversity" in the churches. Other key themes, including justice, spirituality, and mission have presumed some manner of "diversity" (difference) as they have been pursued. In congregations, among regional judicatory leaders, and at denominational headquarters, "diversity" has been a sacred category. It has sparked various educational programs such as antiracism training that have had considerable impact. One former denominational head made "no outcasts" the slogan for his tenure in office. Meanwhile schools, colleges, and seminaries of the various religious bodies have pushed "diversity" to the forefront. Making American religious bodies more racially and culturally diverse has been a widespread obsession.

The intention has been heartfelt. It became part of the religious response to a historic sense of social awakening. The realization in the mid-twentieth century of pervasive discrimination against African-American persons, in the wake of centuries of slavery, shook much of white America. The fact that this realization was so long in becoming widespread, though some black and white leaders had pointed it out for years, was doubly disturbing. As the civil rights movement arose, religious leaders and organizations, black and white, shaped it. The creation of mutual appreciation, and equal opportunity, became intense goals. The matter advanced from overt discrimination to subtler forms in patterns of housing, hiring, and job compensation. The scars of racial bias became clear in social problems that particularly affected black neighborhoods. "Racial profiling" remains a concern as instances of civil authorities treating African-Americans unfairly have become clear. The intention of much of religious America to stamp out racial bias has been well placed and remains an urgent task.

However "diversity" in American life has broadened and the change has been lost on many Americans. No longer can "diversity" be construed only as black and white. For that matter, no longer can American religion be understood as "Protestant-Catholic-Jew" as sociologist Will Herberg depicted over fifty years ago. In a sense, America is awakening to another unfamiliar social reality. Similarly, America must awaken to new patterns of bias and overt discrimination.

A few years ago, ABC News conducted an experiment: a young woman wearing a headscarf, which Muslims call a hijab, went into a local bakery in Texas to purchase a pastry. But she was denied service and insulted as being Muslim by a clerk in the shop. However other customers were unaware that the young woman and the clerk both were actors. ABC News's intention was to gauge the response of other customers. How would onlookers respond in the midst of ugly cultural and religious slurs?

Over the course of a day the scene was replayed as customers came and went. The young woman entered and the clerk insulted her. The results of this experiment were disheartening. A few customers defended her and even scolded the clerk. A few others actually supported the clerk's insults and even joined in making them. Bigotry was masked as the "right to refuse service." But most of the customers did or said nothing. Some stood silently; others left quickly as if to avoid a discomforting situation. They did not know what to do and they did not want to become involved.

No religious census was taken of these customers. But among the more than two dozen, presumably at least a few were members of congregations in this Texas neighborhood. If so, the reality is dismaying. After decades of opposing racism, at least among their religious leaders, the work of congregations is far from done. Only now, that work goes beyond the sort of large-scale events and initiatives that heralded the civil rights era. Now that work focuses on local contexts and on racial, cultural, and religious diversity of greatly expanded scope.

The issue is vexing, and congregations are proving to be inept in addressing it. Part of the reality may be that most of America's congregations still view the world as "Protestant-Catholic-Jew" in a way that was accurate in the mid-twentieth century. Now religious diversity especially leaves many congregations befuddled. One lay leader in a congregation admitted there was a problem. "Diversity is one of our values, what we say we believe," she affirmed. "But look at our pews. We're not diverse at all. We say the right things, but we don't know how to do them."

"Diversity" has indeed been a cherished goal for many congregations, and one they have not lost sight of in the words they utter. It has meant reflecting in their membership the breadth of the neighborhood outside their doors. Steps have been taken in many places and tangible good has resulted. Blacks and whites, as individuals and as congregations, have forged bonds. There has been concerted attention to healing and to addressing social issues together. Practical steps have been taken. Understanding has been built. Clearly things are better.

But the neighborhood outside the doors of most congregations is no longer only black and white. Inviting people to one's pews is no longer an adequate emphasis when those being invited are Muslim or Jewish, Sikh or Hindu, Jain or Buddhist. For that matter, it is even more difficult to invite people like Ashley who want to be fed by multiple religious and spiritual streams at once. Membership, and even participation in the congregation, must take a new turn. For this to happen, congregations must shed a pattern of thinking and acting that is ingrained. They must consider themselves spiritual communities first and religious institutions second.

From Common Institutions to the Common Good

The task of dealing appreciatively with diverse faith communities and faiths has been apparent from America's founding. Once, reaching a peak in the second half of the twentieth century, there was talk of the "ecumenical movement" and "ecumenism." National religious leaders and scholars from theological faculties met to formulate statements of common belief and joint initiative. Arduous efforts enhanced mutual appreciation, especially among America's Christians. Local efforts sprouted in the new light of religious respect. Joint occasions convened various traditions, especially on national holidays such as Thanksgiving and July 4. Good feelings about unity amid diversity spread.

Similarly the realization that America was a varied religious tapestry extended the meaning of "ecumenism" toward fresh emphasis on "dialogue." Protestants, Catholics, and Jews especially gathered nationally and in major cities, uniting leaders and theologians, producing further appreciation. In some cities, "interfaith councils" arose and followed the pattern set by ecumenical activity. In a new vein there were occasional events, perhaps joint statements, and in some instances guidebooks and teachings on major issues as well as local civic concerns. Once again there were good results and deepened understanding. Interfaith groups found they could unite to feed the hungry and house the homeless. There could be counseling and tutoring and job placements services. Much good resulted in situations where good outcomes had been rare. But still something was missing and it was apparent to Ashley.

> A religious man is a person who holds God and man in one thought at one time, at all times, who suffers harm done to others, whose greatest passion is compassion, whose greatest strength is love and defiance of despair.
>
> **Abraham Joshua Heschel**
>
> *The Jewish Experience: An Introduction to Jewish History and Jewish Life,* Steven Leonard Jacobs

As there was increasing zest for spirituality in American life, there was diminished energy for religious institutions. In fact there was little disdain for such institutions, just a growing lack of recognition of them. The services provided by them were more urgently needed than ever, but Ashley's generation had little regard for them if caring for people was dragged through institutional process. Something of the deep essence of faith had to surface, revealing that people, and not institutional structures, could find common ground and create common good together. If faith meant anything, it meant actual people joining in common purpose.

Early in the twenty-first century, tangible signs of such intention surfaced. In 2007 a document issuing a bold call to shared faith and initiative, "A Common Word," was issued by a Jordanian leader. "A Common Word" encouraged Muslims and Christians to join in encouraging love of God and love of neighbor as the key tenets of both faiths and the most faithful response to the world's needs. Out of A Common Word came conferences and conversations on several continents. Hundreds of faith leaders endorsed the document, with Jewish leaders joining their counterparts. A Common Word was a bold breakthrough in interfaith understanding.

Meanwhile, from scholars at the University of Cambridge and the University of Virginia, there arose an effort to encourage interfaith groups to form around discussion of their sacred texts together. Muslims, Jews, and Christians could create ongoing small group discussion of common themes seen through passages from their sacred scriptures. This practice was known as Scriptural Reasoning (SR) and became something of an international movement seen especially in academic contexts and among educated laypersons. The beauty of SR was its capacity to build ongoing bonds across lines that often divide. As we mentioned in chapter five, it is also growing in appeal at the grassroots level as people seek to dig beneath the surface of religious life in search of its spiritual wellsprings.

But somehow a more general appeal was needed, something larger than a small group, but not laden with institutional formalities. What could that be? How could something be organized and gain traction and become ongoing in local contexts? What might have wide appeal and be simple and understood immediately? What could embody basic humanity, and the basic spiritual searches of people like Ashley?

A Simple Beginning: Hospitality

Over lunch one day, a rabbi in a medium-sized metropolitan area raised that question to a group of friends. He had been part of dialogues and he had written position papers on interfaith respect and he had brought people to help with a local shelter program. He had even taken part in an interfaith pilgrimage to the Middle East. He liked what he had heard about Scriptural Reasoning and he was heartened by A Common Word. But how could more people become involved and not have it feel overly formal? How could multiple spiritual searches be guided and encouraged? The rabbi knew this group of friends would have some ideas.

If any group would have ideas, this one would. By pure chance a small group of Jewish, Muslim, and Christian leaders had begun having lunch periodically. There was never an agenda. They liked one another and built a natural level of comfort. Occasionally they had dinner with each other and brought their spouses. The warmth was infectious. Slowly they expanded their group and fresh compatibility resulted. The conversations deepened and moved easily between the serious, the personal, and the lighthearted. Distinctions among them were obvious but did not confine who they were together. They simply enjoyed having meals together with no agenda.

"That's the answer," said the pastor of a large evangelical congregation. "It's about hospitality. We like having fellowship together. All of our faiths talk about hospitality. Let's build on that." The rabbi eagerly responded: "Remember in Genesis 18, Abraham rushed to greet the strangers. Can't we all get our arms around that?" An imam smiled: "I'm always ready to eat. Let's build on what we have." Their smiles now were broad. It was just that simple and that scriptural for each of them: *hospitality*. Just time set aside for a common meal with no agenda and no formal anything.

> Every time we gather becomes a model of the future we want to create.
>
> **Peter Block**
>
> *Community: The Structure of Belonging*

"Amazing," a professor of Jewish Studies said later when he had joined the group for a meal. "You have simply cut through formalities and built fellowship." Where interfaith events had been the prerogative of clergy and academics, the simple emphasis of hospitality opened it to everyone. A meal at a Baptist congregation attracted dozens of people, bringing further confirmation. The only agenda was hospitality. People gathered six to a table at round tables. Soon there was talk of families and children and siblings, work and local issues and tasks all congregational leaders face. There was much to discuss, and nothing was hindered by the real differences that have thwarted other efforts at interfaith understanding.

Ashley lived in a different city from where these gatherings had gained momentum. But she would have been drawn to them. She would have felt at home when a rabbi's wife laughed at a story told by a council member from a nearby Islamic center. She would have felt fascination and some surprise when a Baptist pastor and an imam compared their understandings of religious conversion. Meanwhile Presbyterian and Episcopal clergy compared notes on visits to the Middle East and a young seminary faculty member shared insights on the theological meaning of peace from recent research. Ashley would have felt heartened. This would be the setting in which she could find the spiritual direction she sought. Or was it? As much as she would have gained from such an occasion, it would have intensified an issue that was frustrating her spiritual search. It was an issue that had little to do with any particular congregation or faith tradition, and everything to do with American religious pluralism. How, she wondered, could one find the right spiritual home without disparaging the religious or spiritual affirmations of others? How could she choose one path without negating other paths chosen by others?

Being One among Many

The Reformation reinforced an emerging modus operandi of the church: to be the church is to promote your version of Christianity. Actually, we are putting this in very diplomatic terms. Tragically, "promote" also entailed eradicating your enemies, a.k.a., burning them at the stake! Thankfully, this no longer occurs, though the concept of promoting one's version of Christianity remains. To put this into contemporary terms, one could say churches believe and promote their brand of Christianity to distinguish themselves from one another. The result has been a proliferation of church brands. Consider this: at the turn of the twentieth century there were around two thousand denominations (brands) in the world. Today there are well over thirty thousand! Some celebrate this trend as part of God's movement to create different kinds of churches for different kinds of people. But in our estimation, it has so narrowed an individual church's perspective on faith that it has become too limited to meet the diverse ways people desire to approach faith and practice.

We live in information culture that knows about the diversity of the world and prompts people to seek out diversity as a pathway to personal enrichment, which reflects in where we choose to live. For nearly seventy years, the suburbs, which are quite homogenous communities, have reigned as the place to be. Today, people are moving toward cities and suburbs with an urban edge because they offer more engagement with the diversity around us. What people seek in a church is the same—a place where diverse people are welcomed and diverse approaches are practiced. Yet churches, because of past approaches, have avoided not only the diversity of religions around us, they continue to avoid the diversity we have within the Christian tradition. To the uninitiated youth of our day, the diverse brands of Christianity represent opportunity, not past battles about who is right or wrong.

There is a yearning among many for the church to be able to see its internal diversity as the breadth of resources that the Christian faith offers local congregations. This is why the title of one of Brian McLaren's book struck such a chord: *A Generous Orthodoxy: Why I Am a Missional, Evangelical,*

Post/Protestant, Liberal/Conservative, Mystical/Poetic, Biblical, Charismatic/Contemplative, Fundamentalist/Calvinist, Anabaptist/ Anglican, Methodist, Catholic, Green, Incarnational, Depressed-yet-Hopeful, Emergent, Unfinished CHRISTIAN.[49] This title represents how many now see themselves. And because of the branding the church has done, it also represents why it is such a struggle to find a church that allows a broad pathway in one's spiritual pursuit.

> We must never underestimate our power to be wrong when talking about God, when thinking about God, when imagining God, whether in prose or in poetry. A generous orthodoxy, in contrast to the tense, narrow, or controlling orthodoxies of so much of Christian history, doesn't take itself too seriously. It is humble. It doesn't claim too much. It admits it walks with a limp.
>
> **Brian McLaren**
>
> *A Generous Orthodoxy*

There is a lesson for us about embracing diversity in the formation of our sacred scripture. If we had not embraced the breadth of understandings about Jesus, the Bible might look quite different. In the first three centuries of Christianity, the individual Gospels were circulated among the churches, but often churches only had one of the four Gospels. They built their understandings of Jesus, God, and faith on the Gospel in their possession. As we know, each Gospel has its distinctive character and emphasis, which led to diverse understandings of the Christian faith. The miracle of the canonization of scripture is that the church agreed to include all four Gospels. The church embraced a fourfold witness of Jesus Christ rather than narrowing it to one. This inclusivity has left the church with a perennial struggle about how to

interpret the Gospels because of their differences, but in the
end, the movement of the Spirit prompted us to embrace a
diverse witness rather than a singular one.

Unfortunately, over time we have truncated the diversity
of the Christian faith through our relentless branding, and it
is time to reopen ourselves to the full breadth of our tradition. Otherwise we are limiting the resources that can help us
reach a new cultural context and a new generation. One can
think of this as a cross-pollination of our churches with one
another. We need to share our theologies, liturgies, prayers,
and practices, and expose our people to them—Episcopalian
with Baptist, Presbyterian with Eastern Orthodox, Lutheran
with Moravian. In them we will find stimulating and challenging ideas and practices that can be catalytic in our pursuit of a growing faith.

In our education programs, why not have an Eastern
Orthodox presentation on the notion that Christ became
human so that we might become divine? Why not have a
Moravian share the experience and importance of sharing
sweet buns in worship? Why not have a contemporary church
include ancient prayers, or a liturgical church offer sponta-
neous space in worship? Rather than perpetuating our brands,
we need to seek out the resources others use to nourish their
faith. Let us be clear: in doing so each church must continue
to have a core understanding and approach to faith and life.
But by incorporating the perspectives and practices of others,
we are availing ourselves of all that the Christian tradition
has to offer in meeting the spiritual needs of our people.

Of course, the church being what it is, newcomers will
find this broadened approach liberating and old-timers may
find it frustrating—and will certainly let you know it! But if
it is handled well, it introduces an importance lesson in what
it means to belong, believe, and be the church. To be a place
of belonging means making space for others. Congregations

need to learn that the church's main duty is not to "trip your personal trigger" with every anthem, hymn, prayer, and program. The church's duty is to reach out and make space for the diversity of people that God has created and is calling into community. We need to shape communities where a congregant's first impulse is not to criticize leadership because they didn't like Sunday's musical selection. The members of our communities need to learn to first ask themselves the question: Was this meaningful to others in the service? If it was, then this is to be celebrated.

Believing is not a private journey that separates us from others. God calls us into community. Not just a community, but the community we call "the Church." This is the Church, capital "C," which includes all those who have a relationship with God through Christ. To ignore this is to deprive us, and all those on the fringes seeking God, of the wonderful diversity of people and approaches that God has bound together. Only when we let the Church into our churches, can we become the spiritual place we are called to be and the kind of church people yearn for us to be.

CONCLUSION

Beyond Fitting In

The Barrier of Fitting In

There is no more urgent need today than the need to belong. Often in quiet uncertainty, and occasionally in desperation, many people feel they have no place. They are people of all ages and generations, but young adults are especially unsure. Amid what would seem like an obvious opportunity for service and growth, few congregations respond adequately. While fretting over diminishing numbers and shrinking pools of volunteers, congregations seem fatally distracted. They are incapable or unwilling to adapt in the ways that are needed to create new opportunities to belong. Small wonder the number of religiously unaffiliated people is growing; few congregations are poised to welcome them.

Nancy, who is nearly Ashley's age, equates approaching a congregation with the move to a new city her family made when she was in high school. "The biggest thought on my mind was not getting lost on campus or the classes I was assigned. The biggest concern was where I would sit in the cafeteria at lunch." That's because Nancy saw that she faced various, tightly wound groups of students: athletes, geeks, party goers, school government types, rich kids, poor kids, etc., the variety of an urban public high school was on full display. So where would Nancy, the new kid, belong?

For Nancy this meant more than "fitting in"; she deeply wanted to find a small group with whom she resonated. She wanted to belong. But could this happen? It wasn't simply a matter of choice: She might choose a group but would they choose her? Barely into the ninth grade, Nancy plunged into a desperate search to belong. Now she can look back and manage a slight smile. But then it was painful.

Later, when she had found a congregation where an adult sense of place was possible, Nancy equated that school cafeteria with belonging in a religious sense. "It was like that feeling of so many different groups, none of whom cared whether you were there or not. I'm lucky I connected with a few people and some doors opened. But it wasn't easy."

Nancy was fortunate. For some people, still desperate to belong, the doors will never open. Maria, an immigrant from El Salvador, now makes a decent living through the cleaning service she started. She has succeeded to the point that she has part-time employees. Maria lives with the man who fathered her child and considers herself fortunate—the man has a job and they are together. She wears a small cross around her neck and speaks appreciatively of her faith. But approaching congregations is out of the question. "I would feel out of place," she says wistfully.

In this book we have described the major challenge congregations face today. It is a challenge that will have more lasting consequences than the worries that prove so absorbing now. Concerns over finances and conflicts over social issues, or simply leadership and mission, are symptoms of the larger issue. But little time and effort go into addressing it. The issue of belonging is at the heart of the concerns congregations claim they must address. The issue of belonging also pervades American life. It is not widely understood, much less seen as a deeply religious issue. But its resolution must be framed in religious terms. The issue of belonging ultimately is an issue of meaning and purpose. Belonging concerns the links between people, how the story of an individual life becomes a shared communal story. It also concerns the pursuit of a fulfilling and worthwhile sense of direction that fosters mutual commitment. Belonging is a social issue, whose roots and resolution are religious.

The Move toward Belonging

How then can congregations address it? In this conclusion we want to sketch the contours of an adequate response. We do not claim to have fully shaped answers to the challenge of belonging, nor will we propose a "how-to" solution for congregations. To a great extent, this book is intended to call attention to the problem of belonging and to explain its nature in light of patterns of contemporary congregational life. But the crisis of belonging, for indeed it has become a crisis in American life, is still unfolding in various respects. A generation younger than Ashley's is maturing, with no greater certainty about its sense of place.

Meanwhile immigration is bringing still greater diversity to American society. Mobility and population growth are creating new mixes of people throughout American life. In fact, the crisis of belonging pervades our society; no cities or towns or geographic regions are exempt. All generations feel the impact. Ashley's parents, Carol and Bill, moved to a retirement facility close to where Ashley lived. When they did, she saw their challenges were similar to her own: meeting people, getting oriented to a new location, finding activities they liked. The rapid growth of retirement communities also reveals the issue of belonging: people find themselves in unusual and unprecedented proximity. However, as we have emphasized, proximity alone does little to create a sense of belonging. Somehow, the fabric of community must be knit.

As a result, the meaning of belonging is shifting from an older, static understanding to the presumption of dynamic breadth. To say this is not to speak uncritically, or to simply embrace a major social trend. Congregations in particular must offer religious and moral critiques without distancing themselves and trying to evade the issues raised by this new social phenomenon. Thus the brief, episodic encounters that characterize many lives today frustrate rather than fulfill the search for ways to belong. Ashley would realize that she was seeking to belong in ways that would inherently frustrate her search. She would also realize that she did not know how to belong; a search was necessary if she was going to discover what belonging meant. In ways that can prove painful, she and her peers try to belong in ways that do not last, and may be flawed. Saying that belonging is their intention, they can act in ways that make its realization unlikely. If it means anything, belonging entails continuity and commitment in building a way of life, a reality with which Ashley and others have struggled.

If Christianity was only about finding a group of people to live life with, who shared openly their search for God and allowed anyone, regardless of behavior, to seek too, and who collectively lived by faith to make the world a little more like Heaven, would you be interested?

"Hell yes!" was his reply. He continued. "Are there really churches like that?"

Matt Smay and Hugh Halter

The Tangible Kingdom: Creating Incarnational Community

Ironically congregations face the same possible frustration in similar ways and for comparable reasons. Few congregations declare that they do not want people to attend and to become affiliated. Most congregations readily say they want people to belong. After all, the tenets of faith and the life to which faith points compel attention to belonging. From pulpits, in classes, and even in committees and meetings, heartfelt calls for openness and initiative often ring. But still, more often than not, people in search of belonging feel they are on someone else's turf when they enter a congregation, if they enter at all. It quickly becomes clear that the words uttered in most congregations are flatly contradicted by their lack of adequate welcome. It is not clear that most congregations want to draw people who are unfamiliar to them into belonging, especially when it appears a new approach to belonging is required.

In their defense, congregations face an array of genuine challenges, any one of which demands time and resources. Congregations can say, with justification, that they are distracted. Many face all-consuming situations of conflicts, diminished membership, and deteriorating facilities. But there is a more pervasive challenge, which many congregations overlook in their zeal to deal with symptoms and not causes. There is a deeper question which few congregations address adequately: How can a congregation present a message and an image of faith community that are clear and compelling? In other words, why would anyone want to participate in your congregation? What about your congregation's life is so true and so urgent that people will change their weekend habits to go there? And if people who are new do appear, what does your congregation offer that will make a difference in their lives?

Some leaders of congregations, lay and ordained, sense this challenge and grasp its significance. They quickly add that they must live in at least three different worlds at once. Every congregation must attend to the members it already has, first and foremost. This is their core, the basis of their life, the means of their support. Current members set the tone; they have defined the life of the congregation in the past, perhaps even for decades. They will want to be heard about all aspects of the congregation's life. They come first.

Leaders of congregations must also, in some respect, engage the realities of their locality, that is, the social context in which they are situated. Only a minority of congregations ignore their context, and always at their peril. If nothing else, the congregation's members are affected by what goes on around them. If there is an economic downturn, for instance, or an increase in local crime, or issues with the schools, the congregation feels the impact. Dealing with current members and the neighborhood easily become all consuming.

At the same time congregations must function as a part of a larger, denominational whole. There is a wider faith tradition, and religious institution, that it represents. With conflicts within denominations, and friction about the proper understanding and presentation of faith tradition, congregational leaders often must backpedal, trying to be team players in their confessional worlds, but framing wider issues in ways they can be addressed, or circumvented, in a local context. Given disputes over the Bible, human sexuality, the role of women, social issues, and social justice activism, congregations easily feel swamped by demands they did not invite.

So how much time and energy are left for people whose potential for becoming involved seems slight? The depth of Ashley's search may be genuine and even profound. Perhaps something could be learned from her. But programs have to be run, people need visits and counseling, and there is worship to plan. Ashley could be here today and gone tomorrow, congregation leaders are inclined to think. What good would come from paying inordinate attention to her, when it is not at all clear she would fit in?

Thus many congregation leaders have their emphasis firmly placed on fitting in rather than on belonging in the deep sense Ashley seeks to discover. By such thinking, congregations miss the religious significance in their midst, and they fail to grasp that Ashley and her peers are a growing fixture; their presence is becoming unavoidable. Moreover, Ashley and the younger generation appearing after her have a hunger to belong that would benefit the congregation in all aspects of its life. We emphasize that the opportunity they present is greater than the challenge congregations are inclined to perceive. By responding effectively to them, congregations can also address the issues they more readily perceive. She and her ilk are not a special situation. They epitomize the demands before congregations today. Belonging has become the core issue.

How can congregations embody a lively, faithful approach to belonging that welcomes the people on spiritual journeys, especially younger generations? In this book we have seen that many congregations and leaders are unaware of Ashley, or unable to adapt in ways that would incorporate her. Notably, some leaders and congregations strike the opposite pose: they believe they understand precisely what will attract Ashley. They propose to depict Christianity as broad and modern, in contrast to what they see as the faith's moribund adherence to outdated concepts. Reframing belief in credible, contemporary terms will surely attract people like Ashley, who are turned off by ancient dogmas that are not genuine to the Christian faith.

In the eyes of such theologians and clergy, Christianity in theory and congregations in fact must adapt by reframing belief. Otherwise they face extinction in modern life. The issue is one of credibility. In a sense we agree, though this approach risks becoming ungrounded for the sake of accommodating people who have religious doubts. But this demythologized approach misses the point of belonging. Belief is a key factor; however belonging is the core issue. Rather than waiting for her doubt and her sense of social justice to be embraced, Ashley simply wants to belong. As we have urged, she also wants to believe, which means more than having her ability to doubt matters of belief confirmed. Belonging will offer her the space in which to sort out belief. The two go together intimately, a reality many "progressive" religious leaders miss.

In fact Ashley, like many of her generation, wants to grasp what religious tradition means when it is lived fully, not merely when it is expressed clearly. She doesn't care what certain leaders may do or say to endorse her doubts. She wants to know what they stand for, not what they are against. If it is justice, then what is the religious basis on which they pursue justice? If they allow, or even encourage, doubt, in what way does doubt become expressive of basic faith convictions and the community that upholds them? Thus even the most progressive leaders can frustrate her. They offer little access to belonging or believing as she approaches them.

Muslim leaders in the Middle East and in the United States have said to each of us on various occasions: "We don't want you to become Muslim; we want you to be fully Christian, without apology. Then we are clear about where we stand; then we have something to discuss. Then we have the possibility of cooperation." In a similar way Ashley does not approach leaders or congregations who appear either rigid or halfhearted. She wants to know what a congregation and its leaders stand for, and how they put their words into practice. The apparent readiness to dilute faith is a false way of approaching her, and she scorns it.

The true basis for belonging is not uniformity of belief. In fact, Ashley is wary of any push toward being like-minded. The true nature of belonging is finding common ground in the midst of difference. In fact, she has felt more of a pull toward belonging and belief as she has perceived that belonging can unite people across lines that ordinarily divide. Belonging becomes more than what "inclusion" means, as if some religious leader or some congregation is making room for her, perhaps reluctantly. Instead, Ashley seeks to belong in a way that feels like common ground, like the creation together of a way to be together, grounded in faith. She dares to think that she has something congregations need, something that would benefit them. Her search for a way to belong may be instructive. She hopes there is a congregation somewhere that can guide her, with others, toward a shared journey of spiritual growth and service.

So what, specifically, have we found that Ashley, and the many people like her, could offer to congregations? We have seen that belonging can no longer be presumed, and no longer equated with "fitting in." Belonging has become an urgent quest for many people, especially young adults like Ashley. Further, belonging is not an end in itself. Ashley would rather not belong, and continue to search, than accept what to her is a false way. Thus genuine belonging is dynamic rather than static. Genuine belonging means going somewhere worthwhile in the company of others. It is a voyage of discovery, yet grounded in the beliefs and practices of a historic faith tradition. The interplay between belief and practice becomes crucial. There must be adequate space for spiritual discovery, including forms of worship and prayer, but also study and discussion, as well as service and practical response to human need.

In a word, Ashley's search for belonging requires congregations and religious leaders to be *defined*. They must be clear about who they are, what they intend, and on what basis they pursue it. If it is a shared journey of discovery Ashley seeks, then she demands to know where the journey is going, on what basis, and by what means. She assumes that it is a journey along which different sorts of people and religious experience will not only be encountered but will be affirmed. She needs to be grounded adequately, then to engage different realms of religious and spiritual life on that basis. Thus she forces congregations to be clear about who they are, and to strike an appreciative balance between affirming their faith and grasping the faith of others. Congregations must be clear about what they affirm, and flexible in expressing their convictions.

This means that congregations must attend to their *vocation* in the contemporary world. A historic Christian reference, vocation refers to a sense of calling, based upon one's gifts and talents in relation to the circumstances one faces. For a person or a congregation to live in a way that reflects purpose, there must be a clear sense of vocation. For congregations in particular, this means that the various tasks and the qualities they seek to embody must point in coordinated fashion toward faithful, timely purpose. Vocation is not only the congregation's intention, it is the congregation's expression in practical terms of that intention. Vocation includes the outcome or impact of congregational life, and not merely what congregational leaders believe they are doing. Vocation can never be fulfilled by internal institutional process alone. Vocation can only be judged by its reality for persons who stand outside as well as inside the congregation.

The Gift of Strangers

This emphasis on those outside the circle is historic to Christianity. It is always the stranger who reminds us of what we must be. Congregational life requires, and in some sense must be seen through, the lens of outreach. For instance, if there is job loss resulting from economic downturn in a community, the congregation must respond. Amid natural disaster or homelessness or crime, the congregation must respond. Christianity is an incarnational faith. That is, the Christian belief that God took human form in the person of Jesus makes sacred every aspect of human experience and hallows the response of faithful people to human suffering. As a result, it is in response to concrete human need that Christian intention is fulfilled. When the congregation extends itself beyond its presumed boundaries, its vocation becomes complete.

This outreach is the challenge congregations now face in regard to Ashley and her peers. They are the strangers in the congregation's midst. They are not necessarily suffering as congregations are prone to recognize, but they are struggling and they are searching. There is a deep hunger to belong, and not simply to fit in, among them. They represent more than an opportunity for a new program or committee. They represent a challenge to reframe congregational life that few leaders accept. Yet Ashley and her counterparts represent an increasing minority on the religious landscape, and may *become* the largest minority. While many congregations decline, the Ashleys increase. Sadly, and ironically, congregations have what she wants, if they can only see it.

In a large, urban church, the new minister wondered why the main doors, facing a major street, were rarely opened. New leaders have the opportunity to ask questions, and when he asked why, no lay leader or staff member could offer an explanation. The church had functioned for decades with little use of its main doors. People who came knew to enter by side doors.

"It's time to send a new message," the minister announced. The next Sunday, the doors opened, and after that they did so regularly. There was some trepidation among staff and longtime members. But nothing ominous could be detected.

Rather, symbolically, there was an unprecedented sense of welcome. In similar fashion, literally and symbolically, congregations of all sorts must open their doors anew. Regardless of habit or precedent or multiple distractions, the doors must open, lest they be shut permanently. Quite likely, there are people outside who hope to be welcomed.

Notes

1. Brené Brown, *Daring Greatly: How the Courage to Be Vulnerable Transforms the Way We Live, Love, Parent, and Lead* (Gotham Books, Kindle edition, 2012), 231.
2. Charles E. Van Engen, *God's Missionary People: Rethinking the Purpose of the Local Church* (Baker Academic, 1991).
3. Christian Smith et al., *Lost in Transition: The Dark Side of Emerging Adulthood* (Oxford University Press, Kindle edition, 2011).
4. Ibid., 28, 29.
5. "'Nones' on the Rise: One-in-Five Adults Have No Religious Affiliation," *The Pew Forum on Religion & Public Life* (October 9, 2012), www.pewforum.org/2012/10/09/nones-on-the-rise/.
6. Ibid., 9.
7. Ibid., 48.
8. Nancy Ammerman, "Spiritual But Not Religious? Beyond Binary Choices in the Study of Religion," *Journal for the Scientific Study of Religion*, Volume 52, Issue 2, (2013): 258–278.
9. Richard Yeakley, "Growth stalls, falls for largest U.S. churches," *U.S.A. Today* (February 15, 2011), usatoday30.usatoday.com/news/religion/2011-02-16-church_growth_15_ST_N.htm.
10. Reginald Bibby, *A New Day: The Resilience and Restructuring of Religion in Canada* (Project Canada Books, 2012).
11. "'Nones' on the Rise," 22, 24.
12. Diana Butler Bass, *Christianity After Religion: The End of Church and the Birth of a New Spiritual Awakening* (HarperOne, Kindle edition, 2013).
13. Smith, *Lost in Transition*.
14. Sherry Turkle, *Alone Together: Why We Expect More from Technology and Less from Each Other* (Basic Books, Kindle edition, 2012).
15. Smith, *Lost in Transition*, 21, 22.
16. David Brooks, *The Social Animal: The Hidden Sources of Love, Character, and Achievement* (Random House, Kindle edition, 2012).

17. Martin E. P. Seligman, *Flourish: A Visionary New Understanding of Happiness and Well-being* (Atria Books, 2012).
18. American Religious Identification Survey (ARIS), Trinity College, Hartford, 2008. And "Religion," *Gallup,* www.gallup.com/Poll/1690/religion.aspx.
19. Phyllis Tickle, *The Great Emergence: How Christianity is Changing and Why* (Baker Books, 2012).
20. Saint Augustine, *Confessions* (Oxford University Press, 2009).
21. Brown, *Daring Greatly*, 112–71.
22. Ibid., 195.
23. Ibid., 8.
24. Brené Brown, *The Gifts of Imperfection: Let Go of Who You Think You're Supposed to Be and Embrace Who You Are* (Hazelden, Kindle edition, 2010), 49.
25. David Kinnaman and Gabe Lyons, *Unchristian: What a New Generation Really Things About Christianity . . . And Why It Matters* (Baker Books, 2007), 28.
26. David G. Benner, *Sacred Companions: The Gift of Spiritual Friendship & Direction* (InterVarsity Press, 2002), 35.
27. John Wesley, "May 24, 1738," *The Journal of John Wesley* (Moody Press, 1951).
28. Larry Osborne, *Sticky Church* (Zondervan, Kindle edition, 2008), 80.
29. Edwin H. Friedman, *A Failure of Nerve: Leadership in the Age of the Quick Fix* (Seabury Books, Kindle edition, 1999, 2007), Chapter One.
30. "Survey Explores Who Qualifies As an Evangelical," *The Barna Update* (January 18, 2007), www.barna.org/barna-update/culture/111-survey-explores-who-qualifies-as-an-evangelical#.U0WaHKPD-cM.
31. "Truthiness Voted 2005 Word of the Year," *American Dialect Society (ADS)*, www.americandialect.org/truthiness_voted_2005_word_of_the_year.
32. Kendra Creasy Dean, *Almost Christian: What the Faith of Our Teenagers is Telling the American Church* (Oxford University Press, Kindle edition, 2010), Chapter One.
33. An interview with Tanya Marie Luhrmann by Steven Barrie-Anthony, "Prayer, imagination, and the voice of God—in global perspective," *The Immanent Frame: Secularism, Religion, and the Public Square,* blogs.ssrc.org/tif/2013/03/05/prayer-imagination-and-the-voice-of-god-in-global-perspective/.
34. "Millenials: Confident. Connection. Open to Change," *Pew Research: Social & Demographic Trends* (February 24, 2010), www.pewsocialtrends.org/2010/02/24/millennials-confident-connected-open-to-change/.

35. Monica Hesse, "Millennials vs. Generation X: Squabbles reveal a search for identity," *The Washington Post* (October 30, 2011), www.washington post.com/lifestyle/style/millennials-vs-generation-x-squabbles-reveal-a-search-for-identity/2011/10/27/gIQAZVAVXM_story.html.

36. Marcus J. Borg, *The Heart of Christianity: Rediscovering a Life of Faith* (HarperCollins, Kindle edition, 2009), Chapter Two.

37. Luhrmann, *The Immanent Frame*.

38. Brown, *Daring Greatly*, 231.

39. George Lindbeck, *The Nature of Doctrine: Religion and Theology in a Postliberal Age* (Westminster, 1984; 25th Anniversary Edition, 2009).

40. Ibid., Chapter Two describes what is meant by a "cultural-linguistic" approach.

41. Bryan Berghoef, *Pub Theology: Beer, Conversation, and God.* (Wipf & Stock, Kindle edition, 2012).

42. Lawrence Wright, *Going Clear: Scientology, Hollywood, and the Prison of Belief* (Vintage, 2013).

43. Gabriel A. Almond, R. Scott Appleby, Emmanuel Sivan, *Strong Religion: The Rise of Fundamentalisms around the World* (University of Chicago Press, 2003).

44. Almond et al., *Strong Religion*, 23–89.

45. Courtney Bender, *Heaven's Kitchen: Living Religion at God's Love We Deliver* (University of Chicago Press, 2003).

46. Paul Knitter, *Without Buddha I Could Not Be a Christian* (Oneworld, 2013).

47. ARIS.

48. "Nones," *Pew*; and see Bibby, *A New Day*.

49. Brian D. McLaren, *A Generous Orthodoxy: Why I Am a Missional, Evangelical, Post/Protestant, Liberal/Conservative, Mystical/Poetic, Biblical, Charismatic/Contemplative, Fundamentalist/Calvinist, Anabaptist/Anglican, Methodist, Catholic, Green, Incarnational, Depressed-yet-Hopeful, Emergent, Unfinished CHRISTIAN* (Zondervan, 2004).

Select Bibliography

American Religious and Social Trends

Almond, Gabriel A., Appleby, R. Scott, Sivan, Emmanuel. *Strong Religion: The Rise of Fundamentalisms around the World.* University of Chicago Press, 2003.

Ammerman, Nancy. "Spiritual But Not Religious? Beyond Binary Choices in the Study of Religion." *Journal for the Scientific Study of Religion.* Volume 52, Issue 2 (2013): 258–278.

Barrie-Anthony, Steven. "Prayer, imagination, and the voice of God—in global perspective." *The Immanent Frame: Secularism, Religion, and the Public Square.* blogs.ssrc.org. March 5, 2013.

Bass, Diana Butler. *Christianity After Religion: The End of Church and the Birth of a New Spiritual Awakening.* HarperOne, 2013.

Bender, Courtney. *Heaven's Kitchen: Living Religion at God's Love We Deliver.* University of Chicago Press, 2003.

Bibby, Reginald. *A New Day: The Resilience and Restructuring of Religion in Canada.* Project Canada Books, 2012.

Bibby, Reginald. *Beyond The Gods and Back: Religion's Demise and Rise and Why It Matters.* Project Canada Books, 2011.

Block, Peter. *Community: The Structure of Belonging.* Berrett-Koehler, 2009.

Brooks, David. *The Social Animal: The Hidden Sources of Love, Character, and Achievement.* Random House, 2012.

Brown, Brene. *Daring Greatly: How the Courage to Be Vulnerable Transforms the Way We Live, Love.* Gotham Books, 2012.

Brown, Brene. *The Gifts of Imperfection: Let Go of Who You Think You're Supposed to Be and Embrace Who You Are.* Hazelden, 2010.

Chaves, Mark. *American Religion: Contemporary Trends.* Princeton University Press, 2011.

Dean, Kendra Creasy. *Almost Christian: What the Faith of Our Teenagers is Telling the American Church.* Oxford University Press, 2010.

Eck, Diana. *A New Religious America.* Harper San Francisco, 2002.

Edmondson, Amy. *Teaming: How Organizations Learn, Innovate, and Compete in the Knowledge Economy.* Jossey-Bass, 2012.

Haidt, Jonathan. *The Righteous Mind: Why Good People Are Divided by Politics and Religion.* Vintage Books, 2013.

Hesse, Monica. "Millennials vs. Generation X: Squabbles reveal a search for identity." *The Washington Post.* washingtonpost.com. October 30, 2011.

Huertz, Christopher L. and Pohl, Christine D. *Friendship at the Margins: Discovering Mutuality in Service and Mission.* IVP Books, 2010.

Kinnamon, David and Lyon, Gabe. *Unchristian: What a New Generation Really Thinks about Christianity—and Why It Matters.* Baker Books, 2012.

Knitter, Paul. *Without Buddha I Could Not Be a Christian.* Oneworld, 2013.

Lippy, Charles H. and Williams, Peter W., ed., *Encyclopedia of Religion in America.* CQ Press, SAGE Publications, 2010.

Luhrman, T. M. *When God Talks Back: Understanding the American Evangelical Relationship With God.* Vintage, 2012.

Marty, Martin. *Pilgrims in Their Own Land: 500 Years of Religion in America.* Penguin, 1985.

"Millenials: Confident. Connection. Open to Change," *Pew Research: Social & Demographic Trends. pewsocialtrends.org.* February 24, 2010.

"'Nones' on the Rise: One-in-Five Adults Have No Religious Affiliation." *The Pew Forum on Religion & Public Life.* Pewforum.org. October 9, 2012.

Putnam, Robert D. and Campbell, David E. *American Grace: How Religion Divides and Unites Us.* Simon & Schuster, 2012.

Seligman, Martin E. P. *Flourish: A Visionary New Understanding of Happiness and Well-being.* Atria Books, 2012.

Smith, Christian et al, *Lost in Transition: The Dark Side of Emerging Adulthood.* Oxford University Press, 2011.

Smith, Christian et al. *Soul Searching: The Religious and Spiritual Lives of American Teenagers.* Oxford University Press, 2009.

"Survey Explores Who Qualifies As an Evangelical." *The Barna Update.* barna.org. January 18, 2007.

Tickle, Phyllis. *The Great Emergence: How Christianity is Changing and Why.* Baker Books, 2012.

Turkle, Sherry. *Alone Together: Why We Expect More from Technology and Less from Each Other.* Basic Books, 2012.

Wright, Lawrence. *Going Clear: Scientology, Hollywood, and the Prison of Belief.* Vintage, 2013.

Yeakley, Richard. "Growth stalls, falls for largest U.S. churches." *U.S.A. Today.* usatoday.com. February 15, 2011.

Biblical and Theological Resources

Armstrong, Karen. *A History of God.* Ballantine, 1994.

Armstrong, Karen. *The Case for God.* Anchor, 2010.

Augustine. *Confessions.* Oxford University Press, 2009.

Berghoef, Bryan. *Pub Theology: Beer, Conversation, and God.* Wipf & Stock, 2012.

Cracknell, Kenneth, ed. *Wilfred Cantwell Smith: A Reader.* Oneworld, 2001.

Borg, Marcus. *Meeting Jesus Again for the First Time.* HarperOne, 1995.

Borg, Marcus. *The God We Never Knew: Beyond Dogmatic Religion To A More Authentic Contemporary Faith.* HarperOne, 2006.

Borg, Marcus. *The Heart of Christianity: Rediscovering a Life of Faith.* HarperOne, 2004.

Brenner, David G. *Sacred Companions: The Gift of Spiritual Friendship and Direction.* IVP Books, 2004.

Daniel, Lillian. *When "Spiritual but Not Religious" Is Not Enough: Seeing God in Surprising Places, Even the Church.* Jericho Books, 2014.

Ford, David F. and Pecknold, C. C., ed. *The Promise of Scriptural Reasoning.* Wiley-Blackwell, 2006.

Hays, Richard. *The Moral Vision of the New Testament.* HarperOne, 1996.

Lindbeck, George. *The Nature of Doctrine: Religion and Theology in a Postliberal Age.* Westminster John Knox, 2009.

MacCulloch, Diarmaid. *Christianity: The First Three Thousand Years.* Penguin, 2011.

Martin, Dale B. *New Testament History and Literature.* Yale University Press, 2012.

Martin, Dale B. *The Corinthian Body.* Yale University Press, 1995.

McLaren, Brian D. *A Generous Orthodoxy.* Zondervan, 2006.

McLaren, Brian D. *Finding Our Way Again: The Return of the Ancient Practices.* Thomas Nelson, 2010.

McLaren, Brian D. *Why Did Jesus, Moses, the Buddha, and Mohammed Cross the Road?* Jericho Books, 2013.

Metaxas, Eric. *Amazing Grace: William Wilberforce and the Heroic Campaign Against Slavery.* HarperOne, 2007.

Taylor, Barbara Brown. *Learning to Walk in the Dark.* HarperOne, 2014.

Wesley, John. *The Journal of John Wesley.* Oxford University Press, 1987.

Congregational Life Today

Friedman, Edwin H. *A Failure of Nerve: Leadership in the Age of the Quick Fix.* Seabury Books, 1999, 2007. Kindle edition.

Hooks, Bell. *Teaching Community: A Pedagogy of Hope.* Routledge, 2003.

McNeal, Reggie. *Missional Communities: The Rise of the Post-Congregational Church.* Jossey-Bass, 2011.

McNeal, Reggie. *Missional Renaissance: Changing the Scorecard for the Church.* Jossey-Bass, 2009.

Myers, Joseph R., *Organic Community: Creating a Place Where People Naturally Connect.* Baker Books, 2007.

Myers, Joseph R. *The Search to Belong: Rethinking Intimacy, Community, and Small Groups.* Zondervan, 2003.

Osborne, Larry. *Sticky Church.* Zondervan, 2008.

Robinson, Anthony. *Changing the Conversation: A Third Way for Congregations.* Eerdmans, 2008.

Sachs, William L. *In The Face of Difference: Congregations Promoting Understanding and Cooperation.* Rowman & Littlefield, 2014.

Sachs, William L. and Holland, Thomas. *Restoring The Ties That Bind: The Grassroots Transformation of the Episcopal Church.* Church Publishing, 2003.

Smay, Matt and Halter, Hugh. *The Tangible Kingdom: Creating Incarnational Community.* Jossey-Bass, 2008.

Stanley, Andy. *Creating Community: Five Keys to Building a Small Group Culture.* Multnomah Books, 2004.

Stanley, Andy. *Deep and Wide: Creating Churches Unchurched People Love to Attend.* Zondervan, 2012.

Steinke, Peter. *A Door Set Open: Grounding Change in Mission and Hope.* Rowman & Littlefield, 2010.

Steinke, Peter. *Congregational Leadership in Anxious Times: Being Calm and Courageous No Matter What.* Rowman & Littlefield, 2006.

Steinke, Peter, *Healthy Congregations: A Systems Approach.* Rowman & Littlefield, 2006.

Van Engen, Charles E. *God's Missionary People: Rethinking the Purpose of the Local Church.* Baker Books, 1991.

Warren, Rick. *The Purpose Driven Life: What on Earth Am I Here For?* Zondervan, 2013.

Wuthnow, Robert. *Boundless Faith: The Global Outreach of American Churches.* University of California Press, 2010.